CALLED OUT

CALLED OUT

100 Devotions for LGBTQ Christians

E. Carrington Heath

WJK WESTMINSTER
JOHN KNOX PRESS
LOUISVILLE • KENTUCKY

First edition
Published by Westminster John Knox Press
Louisville, Kentucky

22 23 24 25 26 27 28 29 30 31—10 9 8 7 6 5 4 3 2 1

Book design by Erika Lundbom
Cover design by Lisa Buckley Design

Library of Congress Cataloging-in-Publication Data

Names: Heath, E. Carrington, author.
Title: Called out : 100 devotionals for LGBTQ Christians /
 E. Carrington Heath.
Description: First edition. | Louisville, Kentucky : Westminster John
 Knox Press, [2022] | Includes index. | Summary: "One hundred
 devotions on such topics as authenticity, coming out, relationships,
 chosen family, religious trauma, and more to nurture the faith of our
 LGBTQ siblings and help friends, family, and allies grow in under-
 standing and faith"—Provided by publisher.
Identifiers: LCCN 2022034311 (print) | LCCN 2022034312 (ebook) |
 ISBN 9781646982684 (ebook) | ISBN 9780664265724 (paperback)
Subjects: LCSH: Christian sexual minorities--Religious life. | Devotional
 literature.
Classification: LCC BV4596.G38 (ebook) | LCC BV4596.G38 H43
 2022 (print) | DDC 242/.60866 23/eng/20220--dc20
LC record available at https://lccn.loc.gov/2022034311
LC ebook record available at https://lccn.loc.gov/2022034312

Most Westminster John Knox Press books are available at special
quantity discounts when purchased in bulk by corporations,
organizations, and special-interest groups. For more
information, please e-mail SpecialSales@wjkbooks.com.

To Heidi,
through whom the love of God shines.

CONTENTS

CALLED OUT

Chapter 1

CHOSEN FAMILY

When Jesus saw his mother and the disciple whom he loved standing beside her, he said to his mother, "Woman, here is your son." Then he said to the disciple, "Here is your mother." And from that hour the disciple took her into his own home.

—John 19:26–27

In his bleakest hour, when death was close at hand, Jesus was still giving life by doing something extraordinary: creating families.

We know that families are not made by blood, but rather by love. Parents and children open their hearts to one another in adoption all the time. Jesus reminds us, though, that new families can be created at any age in a multitude of ways.

Jesus looks at John, his beloved disciple, and at his mother. And in the moment before his death, he gives them to one another. He binds them together as a new family, responsible to and for one another, even after he is gone.

In the queer community, we create family too. Sometimes out of necessity, as when our families reject us, and sometimes because we are just so great that we can't imagine life without the others we love always being a part of it.

A straight friend of mine, estranged from her abusive family, once told me that the best thing the queer community had ever taught her was that we can have families of choice. We didn't create chosen families—Jesus shows us that. But I do think we just might do them better than anyone else in our culture. It's one of our exports—a gift we can give to the world around us.

For so many, family is a loaded term, fraught with pain and rejection. But it doesn't have to be. One of the queerest things we can do is, conveniently, one of the most Christian: create a family of the people you love, and the ones who also love you. It doesn't matter if it's bound by blood, or by law, or by love.

The people who Jesus would look at with love and say, "You all go together"? That's your family.

Prayer

God, thank you for my family. Both the ones I love who love me, and the ones out there that I haven't even met yet. Amen.

Chapter 2

WADING IN

*They said to Moses, "Was it because there
were no graves in Egypt that you have taken us
away to die in the wilderness? What have you
done to us, bringing us out of Egypt?"*

—Exodus 14:11

When the people of Israel were trapped between
Pharoah's army and the Red Sea, they weren't particularly pleased with Moses. "We had graves back in
Egypt," they shouted, sure that they were about to be
killed. Moses told them not to be afraid, all the while
calling out himself to God for help.

But God calls back, "Why are you crying out to
me? Tell the people to go ahead and go!"

Easier said than done. This wasn't a small creek,
and I'm not so sure everyone knew how to swim. But
the legends passed down by Jewish rabbis tell us that
one man, a guy named Nachshon, dared to stick his
foot in the water. And then, he stuck in his whole leg.
Then his torso. Then his neck. He kept going until the
water was up to his nose, and only then did it begin
to part.

There are times when we stand between the forces
of death and the deepest sea, trying to decide what
to do. That's when God calls back, "What are you

4

waiting for? Dip your toes in the water, and then keep going. I'm waiting for you in the waves, ready to carry you safely across."

Prayer

God, help me to step into the waters of your love, even when I am terrified. Amen.

Chapter 3

SET FREE

"And you will know the truth,
and the truth will make you free."

—John 8:32

I was an adult before I learned that quote was from Jesus. Most people learn this Scripture in church; I learned it from my father who was a CIA officer and taught it to me as his agency's motto. He also was quick to quote it to me when he sensed some equivocation on my part. The implications were clear: "Tell me the truth, and you have nothing to fear. Lie to me, and we're going to have problems."

My dad was the kind of guy my friends both liked and feared a little. Even still, he was one of the first people I told I was gay, back in 1994. Despite his background, much to my surprise, he was also my biggest supporter. He told me that there would be people who would try to think less of me because of who I was, but I couldn't accept that. I had to be who I was, and the world would adjust.

Later, I realized that his response made sense for a man who dealt in secrets. He saw the destructive power that they can have when we try to hide our own truths. He also saw that people who lived without secrets were less apt to be threatened into silence or forced to compromise to survive. He wanted something better for me.

And, like any good parent, I believe God does too.

Prayer

God, help me to find freedom from the tyranny of secrecy. Amen.

Chapter 4

BUTTONED DOWN

Above all, love each other deeply, because love covers over a multitude of sins.

—1 Peter 4:8 NIV

I'm told that on our wedding day, right before the ceremony began, a key button fell off the back of my wife's dress. She did not know this because her matron of honor, our close friend, did some intrepid maneuvering just before the organ prelude began, and cinched the fabric closed.

I've always been incredibly grateful to her for not burdening Heidi with that particular crisis right before we exchanged vows. After all, we were about to do something extraordinarily foolhardy. We were about to stand before people we loved and promise to love one another for the rest of our lives, in sickness and in health, and in just about any other condition you could find. Not only that, but we'd written our own additional vows with even more promises, many of which we invariably break on a weekly basis.

So, the button? It was the last distraction we needed in the moment. But in another sense, that moment when one friend helped another friend not to sweat the small stuff has come back to me again and again.

When we have some minor crisis, one that feels big in the moment but is about as significant as a faulty button, I remember that I don't have to let it distract me from the big picture: At the end of the day, I love her, and she loves me, and we are in this thing together. When I can focus on that, I know that nothing can ruin the day so long as she still wants to walk by my side.

Prayer

God, when little things seem big, may the grandness of love overshadow it all. Amen.

Chapter 5

PROPHETS OF CRUMBS

She said, "Yes, Lord, yet even the dogs eat the crumbs that fall from their masters' table."

—Matthew 15:27

Jesus told a Canaanite woman who was looking for healing for her daughter that he would not help her because, "It is not fair to take the children's food and throw it to the dogs" (Matt. 15:26). In other words, she wasn't Jesus's target audience. I'm going to put aside all the scholarly interpretations of this text that tell you why Jesus wasn't being a complete jerk here and focus on what really matters: that woman and her courage.

Her daughter needed healing. She needed it enough that her mother crossed over the lines of gender, race, and religion and found hope in a man who just might have a solution. And yet when she asked for help, he responded in the most unjust, hope-crushing manner imaginable.

I would have been gone at that point. Forget this guy and his prejudices; who needs him anyhow? But that Canaanite woman wouldn't budge. She stood face-to-face with him and said, "But even dogs get the crumbs."

She wasn't calling herself a dog. I think she was shaming Jesus for his shameful words. She was reminding him that she was a child of God too, not an animal, and that she deserved not just the crumbs, but the full meal.

Jesus heard her, praised her faith, and healed her daughter. That's not the real miracle of this text, though. The real miracle is that woman who dared to speak up and confront injustice. Without her, nothing changes.

Prayer

God, make me a miracle today, that I might make miraculous change in this world. Amen.

Chapter 6

ANCESTORS

*Therefore, since we are surrounded by so great a
cloud of witnesses, let us also lay aside every weight
and the sin that clings so closely, and let us run
with perseverance the race that is set before us.*

—Hebrews 12:1

In the early morning of June 28, 1969, the New York
Police Department, as they had so many other times,
raided the bar. That was nothing new. What was new
was that in a moment of staggering resistance to a
world that hated LGBTQ people, a group of trans and
queer folks decided enough was enough. The Stonewall Riots are marked by many as the flashpoint of
the modern LGBTQ civil rights movement.

It is said that as the police began rounding up club
patrons to arrest, Stormé DeLarverie, a 47-year-old
person of color who has been described as everything
from a "butch lesbian" to a "drag king," handcuffed
and bleeding from an officer-inflicted head wound,
looked up at the crowd and shouted, "Why don't you
guys do something?" Reports say that when Stormé
was then shoved into a police van, the crowd finally
decided to do something they'd never done before:
fight back.

Eight days earlier, Neil Armstrong had stepped foot on the moon, becoming the first person to ever do so. Everyone around the world knew his name, as they should. Armstrong's moon walk would open up new opportunities for the world. But it would be nearly 42 years before I would learn the name of Stormé DeLarverie, who in that same month had done something that would open up new opportunities for me, and for queer and trans folks everywhere, in every bit as radical a way. The shout from the door of a police van left an imprint as deep as a boot on the surface of the moon.

In the summer of 2019, as the fiftieth anniversary of Stonewall approached, the New York Police Department apologized for its actions that night. Stormé, who died in 2014, wasn't around to see it. Part of me wonders whether Stormé would have even accepted that apology. Who knows? But one thing I do hope Stormé would accept is my thanks. Because without that call to the crowd, without that moment of witness, the life I live now, one of opportunity and joy, might have felt just as distant as the moon once did.

Prayer

Dear God, thank you for the witnesses who have gone before us. May they shine as bright as rockets in our memories. And may we always "do something" for the ones who come next. Amen.

Chapter 7

HATED

> *"If the world hates you, be aware that it hated me before it hated you. . . . If they persecuted me, they will persecute you."*

> —John 15:18–20

No one wants to be hated. Not really. We might shrug it off and say we don't really care, but deep down the idea that someone truly despises us is unsettling.

And yet, if you are reading this book, chances are pretty good that someone hates you. I don't mean "you" specifically. You are probably a very nice person. But if you are some variation of LGBTQ, or you care about us, that's good enough to be hated in the minds of some.

People hate what they fear. It's one reason Jesus was hated enough to wind up on a cross. Why? Because Jesus was stirring up trouble, undercutting the religious authorities and, most dangerously, spreading hope. And so, the powers that be killed him. Simply put, Jesus was too powerful to be allowed to live.

He did live, of course. Yes, he died, but death was not the last word. In the end all the hatred and violence of the world did not get the final word. God's love and hope won the day.

When I came out, it was the hatred of people of faith that hurt me the most. Even when it was couched in those soft-sounding code words like "love the sinner, hate the sin," I knew it was still just well-wrapped hatred. A new Christian myself when I came out, I began to wonder if I had made the wrong choice in being baptized. Surely this wasn't what the gospel meant. And if it was, I wanted no part of it.

All these years later, the church has changed. Kids who grew up in the churches that hated people like me are now adults who work for the inclusion of all. I'm glad. But there are days when I wonder whether being hated by a large segment of society actually made me a better Christian. Don't get me wrong; I don't want to go back there. But, early on in my faith life, I had to come to terms with the fact that following Jesus sometimes meant being hated.

Learning how to live with it and find my worth in Christ's love rather than the world's inoculated me against the hatred that the world has for anyone who stands up against the powers that be. On the days when the life of faith is hard, I remember that even Jesus was hated into the ground. And then I remember that in the end that hatred was so weak that, quite literally, it could not keep him down.

Prayer

God, I pray that no one hates me. But if they do, I know that I am in good company, and I know that with you, I rise. Amen.

Chapter 8

CROSSING THE ROAD

"But a Samaritan, as he traveled, came where the man was; and when he saw him, he took pity on him. He went to him and bandaged his wounds, pouring on oil and wine. Then he put the man on his own donkey, brought him to an inn and took care of him. . . . Which of these three do you think was a neighbor to the man who fell into the hands of robbers?"

—Luke 10:33–36 NIV

During the early, fear-filled years of the AIDS crisis, HIV-positive patients experienced heartbreaking discrimination even in their hospital beds. Medical professionals, those who theoretically should have more knowledge and compassion than the general public, were loath to touch those with AIDS. It was as if those who were infected bore a giant scarlet letter.

In the parable of the Good Samaritan, Jesus talks about a man who is traveling when he is robbed and left for dead on the side of the road. As he lays there, two men from his own community, religious officials at that, cross the road to avoid him, and leave him there without help.

It is not until a Samaritan sees the dying man that anyone dares to cross the road and help him. The Samaritan binds up his wounds, takes him to an inn, nurses him to health, and tells the innkeeper to keep him there on the Samaritan's own tab until he finally heals.

Jesus asks which of the three men was the neighbor to the dying man? And the answer is clear: the Samaritan.

It's a call to compassion, one that reminds us to cross the road, even when we are afraid, and to extend care to those in need. And yet, that's not the most radical part of this story. The most radical part is that it is a Samaritan, a member of a group the dying man likely looked down upon, who was a neighbor to that man in need.

To put it in other terms, it isn't just a doctor going into the room of a man with AIDS in 1988 and daring to touch him. Instead, it would be like the man with AIDS crossing the road to save the life of a rabid homophobe who thought AIDS was a just punishment for a "life of sin."

There will always be those who fear us without reason. And yet, they cannot define us. Most of us know what it is to lay on the side of the road in need. Because of that, we will not allow another to do the same. And that, our character, no matter what they call us, is what will define us.

Prayer

God, give me compassion for others, even when they might not give the same to me. Amen.

Chapter 9

FIERCE

I praise you, for I am fearfully and wonderfully made.
Wonderful are your works; that I know very well.

—Psalm 139:14

I had just turned 22 when I started seminary. Fresh out of college, I was young, naive, and unsure of myself. The church at that time, even the most liberal branches of it, was unsure of people like me. Wandering the halls of seminary, I wondered if I had made a mistake. Had God really called this queer and gender-creative young person, just a few years removed from my teenage years, to the ministry?

I turned to my mentor, who was a generation older than me and also gay and a minister herself, for guidance. Together we decided to mark my transition into seminary through a brief ceremony reaffirming my baptism. That day, she held my own worship book in her hands, looked down, and read from this Psalm.

I'm not sure if I had ever heard Psalm 139 before. If I had, I hadn't taken it in. But on this day, the words found my heart: "Fearfully and wonderfully made." Created by God. Made to be exactly who I was, and sent into this world to fulfill this calling as I am.

Over two decades later, every time I read this Psalm I think back to that day. Was it a cure-all? Did my fear and uncertainty leave me all at once? Was I suddenly able to live without self-doubt, confident beyond measure? No. It would be a journey of years, one that some days I'm still on.

But it was a start.

Recently I preached a sermon on this Psalm to my congregation. I wanted to explain what it meant to be "fearfully and wonderfully made." It was that "fearful" word that I knew would trip people up. And so, though I am far from a Hebrew scholar, I went back to the original root of the word.

What I found is that the "fearfully" of Psalm 139, could be better translated today as something like this: fierce. In other words, long before *RuPaul's Drag Race* and *Queer Eye*, God was calling you "fierce." That means that God is also calling you into the world, in all your created wonderfulness, to be fierce.

And so, that's your job for today. Go, and be fierce. This world could use some fierceness. After all, it's just how God made you.

Prayer

Creator God, I pray to you because I am fierce, and I know it. Amen.

Chapter 10

FIGHT ON

Fight the good fight of the faith; take hold of the eternal life, to which you were called and for which you made the good confession in the presence of many witnesses.

—1 Timothy 6:12

In the church, we are sometimes a little too good at defining others by rigid categories. I'm not even talking about identities like race or gender or sexual orientation (though we would still do well to let others define themselves). I'm talking about things like our Enneagram types.

I am, according to my wife, an Enneagram 8. She tells me that this means I am a "challenger," someone who doesn't shy away from confronting injustice, and who loathes the control of others. As I told my wife, I didn't need a test to tell me that.

I prefer to think of it this way: I'm someone who takes "fighting the good fight" seriously. Now, I'm not someone who advocates violence. I've never thrown a punch in my life. But I believe in standing up for what is right and I'm willing to risk rocking the boat if need be.

Sometimes in the church, people like me get a bad rap. We are told we are "contrarians" or that we are somehow creating unrest. In the worst moments, we might be labeled with that worst of all church epithets: unchristian.

But here's the thing: I'm now able not only to be a member of a church in good standing, but to even serve as a pastor in that church because somewhere along the line people like me stood up and rocked the boat. Women, queer folks, trans folks. They had had enough of sitting below deck, told to just be grateful they were allowed onboard. They knew they had gifts that were being wasted down in steerage.

The word this passage uses for "fight" can also be translated like this: to struggle, to race, or to contend. It's not about throwing punches or knocking one another to the ground. It's about caring enough about something to be willing to risk disturbing the peace for it.

There will be times when you will be told to be quiet. Maybe you'll be able to feel others getting frustrated with you and wishing that you would just "let it go." And, maybe there will be times when that is the right thing to do, but no fight for justice or equality was ever won by being more concerned about making friends with certain people while other people were still suffering. After all, when they call you "contentious," it literally means you are caring enough to contend.

That's why sometimes, as hard as it is, we must choose to fight the good fight instead.

Prayer

God, make me a fighter, not for myself, but for all of your children. Amen.

Chapter 11

THE GIFT OF PRIDE

*Pride goes before destruction,
and a haughty spirit before a fall.*

—Proverbs 16:18

Conservative Christians sometimes level judgments at LGBTQ Pride events based on name alone. Pride, they argue, is one of the "seven deadly sins," after all. (Never mind that the list is a completely human-made invention.) To be proud is to prepare for your own fall, Scripture tells us.

If we think about pride in the traditional sense, maybe that's true. The proud person seems boastful, self-assured, and strident. They value themselves more than others, and think they possess a sort of specialness that elevates them above the crowd. When they do fall, whether we admit it or not, there might even be a certain sense of schadenfreude on our parts.

The theologian Paul Tillich argued that pride was the occasion for all sin. And, if you're talking about the kind of pride that lacks humility and denies the humanity of others, perhaps that's true. But in the late 20th century, feminist theologians, aware of the ways women are subjugated, pushed back. For women, they argued, it was not an abundance of pride that kept them from becoming who God had created them to be. Instead, it was the exact opposite.

For LGBTQ people, as well as for any others who have traditionally been denied their full dignity, pride is a radical claiming of God's image in us. When we feel pride in who we are, including our queerness or transness, we are more capable of living into God's plans for us in the world. For us pride is not hubris. Pride is the exact opposite of that.

That's because true pride is not a belief that you are better than anyone else. True pride is an understanding that God has made you just as wonderfully as everybody else. True pride is understanding that you have important work to do in this world, and that being queer or trans is not a barrier to this work. Instead, it is part of the tools that God has given you to do the work of your life.

Prayer

God, I have a lot of work to do today. Thank you for the tools you have given me to do it. May I be proud enough to use every single one. Amen.

Chapter 12

ELDERS

The teaching of the wise is a fountain of life.

—Proverbs 13:14

A friend of mine is eighteen years older than me, just about a full generation older. I met her as a confused 20-year-old kid, both newly Christian and newly out, and still trying to figure out how I could be both. I met her for the first time having no idea that she was both queer and Christian as well.

She's been a guide for me for more than two decades. In college, she helped me buckle down enough to graduate. In seminary, she asked the big questions that helped me see where God was leading me. Even now, if I get stuck on some challenge in my work as a pastor, I know I can pick up the phone and get some good advice from her.

Along the way she's encouraged me, affirmed me, and believed in me. But that's not to say that she's always been easy on me. She's always been the first to tell me when I've gone in the wrong direction, and the first to remind me to get back on the right path.

I got frustrated with her early on in our relationship and asked, "Why are you so hard on me?"

I can't remember her exact response, but I do remember the meaning. She held me to higher standards not because she was mean or punishing. She did it because she cared about me and wanted me to grow into the person God had created me to be.

Everyone needs guidance from time to time, especially from someone a little ahead of us on the path of life. At the same time, it can be tempting to stay away from someone who will call us to account. Being told to stop making excuses and do the right thing can be hard to hear. But, when it's done by someone who cares enough about you to tell you the truth, their words can become a fountain of life.

The trick is finding the right people to fill that role. What no one tells you is that you get to pick your own elders. You don't have to take advice from every person willing to give it to you unsolicited. You can look for people you can respect who will also respect you; those who live their lives with an integrity you want to recreate in your own life. Eventually, even on the days they challenge you, you'll be glad that they're there.

Prayer

God, bring true elders into my life, people who will tell me the truth and lift me up along the way. Amen.

Chapter 13

GRAPPLING

Jacob said, "I will not let you go, unless you bless me."

—Genesis 32:26b

When I was in seminary, I decided to start taking judo classes at a local dojo. Like most people my age who were born female, my official participation in contact sports was prohibited when I was growing up. I loved playing tackle football or wrestling with neighborhood boys and was sad when they got to head off to the high school teams that allowed them to keep playing.

Me? I headed off to the golf team, perhaps the least contact sport ever.

So, when at 22 I found myself grappling on the mats at the dojo, it felt both familiar and forbidden. But I gave it a try. I convinced one of the stronger black belts to teach me how to win a match on the mats. Equally matched for weight, I would use all my strength to try to pin him down. He would simply flip me back onto my back and tell me to try again.

Scripture tells us that Jacob was alone one night in the wilderness. A man came and began wrestling with him. All through the night, to the dawn, they grappled. Then the man said, "Let me go, for the day is breaking" (Gen. 32:26a). But Jacob would not stop wrestling until the man blessed him.

Sometimes my relationship with God has felt like a pleasant walk through the world, side by side and peaceful. But other times it's felt as hard as those grappling matches back at the dojo. Every time I think I've got God pinned down this time, God somehow manages to get the upper hand.

I don't think God is a bully, who throws around God's weight to defeat us. Instead, I think God loves us enough to get down on the mats with us, and to let us keep trying and striving. I think that somehow God respects that. In fact, I think God respects it enough, that God blesses us when we care enough to stay in the struggle.

Prayer

God, on the days when I go to the mat with you, please don't leave me without a blessing. Amen.

Chapter 14

A LONG PARADE

I consider that the sufferings of this present time are not worth comparing with the glory about to be revealed to us.

—Romans 8:18

Somewhere in a box at the back of my closet is a picture from the summer I was 19. A small group of us, fewer than ten or so, were marching by Piedmont Park in the Atlanta Pride parade. We represented our local university; our group consisted of all the students, staff, faculty, and alums who dared to march.

We felt pretty good about having almost ten. It was a record turnout.

Later that school year, Atlanta would be gripped by a series of bombings, including one at a lesbian bar. My friends and I flooded into the bars the next night, on high alert for stray backpacks or packages. By our presence we were saying that our community wouldn't be intimidated by those who hated us.

This morning I opened my Instagram account and saw a series of photos posted by my alma mater's official account. In picture after picture, different groups of students, undeterred by the rain and accompanied by the school's costumed mascot, marched through downtown Atlanta. I couldn't even count how many were there.

I believe God calls us to be courageous in the struggle. Not just for ourselves but for the future.

The work is far from done, but seeing that so many young people who inhabit the same spaces I once did now feel free to come out is a testament to the fact that one generation paves the way for the next. The struggles of my generation compelled us to make it easier for the next, just as the struggles of the generations before mine made it possible for even the ten of us to be marching freely down that street over twenty years ago.

I wonder what Pride pictures will look like twenty years from now. Will those students look back at the pictures from recent years and wonder about what it was like to be queer in an era when the rights of LGBTQ people were under a fresh round of attacks? Will they realize that in a time of struggle, those young people were marching for them?

We all stand on the backs of those who have struggled for us. And God calls us to be ladders to glory for those who come next.

Prayer

God, just as others have struggled for me, help me to struggle for others. In this, you are glorified. Amen.

Chapter 15

NO LONGER

There is no longer Jew or Greek, there is no longer slave or free, there is no longer male and female; for all of you are one in Christ Jesus.

—Galatians 3:28

A few years ago, I had a Sunday off from my church and went with a friend to their church. This was a well-known progressive church, one that prominently signaled its welcome to LGBTQ people with signs outside of the doors and had taken care to emphasize that they welcomed trans folks. My friend and I are both gender non-binary, so this was especially important to us.

That's why we were so surprised by what happened during the service. During a call-and-response reading, the congregation was broken up into "men" and "women" with the two groups reading alternating lines. My friend and I stood and said nothing. Forced into a false binary, we weren't sure what line we were supposed to read.

Paul wrote to the Galatian church that in Christ the false binaries of the world are transcended. Jew or Greek. Slave or free. Male or female. Instead, we are all worthy, equal, and united in Christ. For all the ways Paul gets it wrong sometimes, two thousand years later these particular words are still radical and right.

That's why non-binary genders shouldn't be as perplexing to the church as they seem to be. After that Sunday, my friend tried to educate the pastors on why the language was problematic. They tried again when a song was divided into "men" and "women" a few months later. Staff members, some of whom were gay, told them, "I don't see what the big deal is." When it kept happening, they finally gave up on the church.

The world does its best to force us into false binaries. For some people, the binary choices fit just fine. And that's great. But for others, their truth is a little more nuanced.

Being a part of the body of Christ should mean that the church that surrounds you will take the time to get to know you and to understand you in all your beautiful complexity. When you have the courage to share yourself at your deepest level, the church should say, "This is how God created you, and so we want to understand the particular beauty of God's creation as embodied in you."

It won't always be done perfectly. We're all human, and we're all learning. But if you are in a place where you are not being understood, it is OK to find a place where you will be. God's wonderful creation deserves nothing less.

Prayer

God, help me to see past false binaries, and help me to honor the complex beauty that you create. Amen.

Chapter 16

HUMBLE

God has told you, O mortal, what is good; and what does the LORD require of you but to do justice, and to love kindness, and to walk humbly with your God?"

—Micah 6:8

Years ago, a clergy friend of mine had the unenviable task of eulogizing her own father. He had been, by all accounts, a good man. He'd loved his family, worked hard, practiced his faith, and been a community leader. She picked this verse because she saw it as an encapsulation of how he had chosen to live his life.

I was in my twenties at the time, and I was struggling with the idea of what it meant to "walk humbly." Like most queer and trans people, after growing up in a culture that told me that people like me should not be proud, I was just learning to feel good about myself. Pride was a new and powerful feeling.

So, humility? It felt a little like going back in the closet.

What I came to understand, though, was that having humility is not the same as being humiliated. Being humiliated is an act of violence. It's another person robbing you of your rightful pride. But being humble? That's a choice you get to make about how you treat everyone else in the world.

Humility is not a sort of mousy acquiescence to others. That's just being a doormat. Instead, true humility can only come when you understand that you are good and beloved by God, and that you deserve to be treated that way. True humility also means that we understand that others are good and beloved by God, and that they deserve to be treated that way too. The most truly accepting and affirming people I know are also some of the most self-assured, in the best sense of that word. And some of the meanest, most judgmental, are some of the most unhappy with themselves. They can't have the kind of humility that treats others with respect because they've never found that kind of respect for themselves.

I think about my friend who buried her father all those years ago. She's one of the strongest people I know. She's also one of the most humble. She leads her life with a quiet dignity that draws respect from others, and she treats everyone she meets with respect. I think her father would be proud of her.

Humility is an underrated virtue in our world. Humility doesn't win elections or get attention. But true humility, the kind that lifts people up to your own level rather than crushes you down, just might be what we need to transform the fractured ego of our world.

Prayer

God, help me to be humble, not so that I am less but so that all are more. Amen.

Chapter 17

AFRAID OF GOD?

The fear of the LORD is the beginning of wisdom.

—Proverbs 9:10

Recently a parishioner shared one of his favorite Bible verses with me: "The fear of the Lord is the beginning of wisdom."

I don't know if he noticed, but I recoiled a little. It sounded like God was a little "smitey."

Later, I spent some time with that text. I looked up what the Hebrew word for "fear" here really meant. And I found, to my disappointment, that indeed it did mean "fear." But digging deeper I found that it wasn't the kind of terror of a damning God that too many Christians, especially queer Christians, are taught growing up.

Instead, this is about awe. It's about seeing God so clearly that we can't help but express our amazement. It's like standing on the edge of the Grand Canyon, or looking up at a star-filled sky, and realizing the majesty and awesomeness of what is before us. And then it's realizing that the Creator of all those things must be even more majestic and more awesome than all of creation.

When I try to comprehend God's greatness, I am reminded of what comes first. It puts the world in perspective. It is the start of all wisdom because it is the firm foundation of everything else that I know. And, yes, a God that wonderful is also a little terrifying, the same way that looking up at the night sky and seeing stars light-years away can be terrifying. But to be loved fiercely by a God that awesome? That's amazing too.

I sometimes think that's why we push so hard for the rights of all. We fear God, in the best sense of the word. We are in awe of God, and so we are in awe of God's good creation, including God's LGBTQ children. It's that wisdom that creates true passion for justice in the church.

Prayer

God, sometimes you are so great that I am afraid. On those days, give me the wisdom to know that you do not wish to frighten us, but only to make us great too. Amen.

Chapter 18

CASTING OUT FEAR

There is no fear in love, but perfect love casts out fear; for fear has to do with punishment, and whoever fears has not reached perfection in love.

—1 John 4:18

On the day my wife Heidi and I were married, one of our closest friends read from this passage at our wedding.

Heidi and I had both grown up in a dominant culture that taught that our love was wrong. For my wife, who left her Episcopal upbringing for a more conservative evangelical group in college, during the same time she was falling in love for the first time, those teachings were especially damaging.

When the local pastor who supervised her college fellowship found out that she was gay, he removed her from her leadership position in the group. He told her that her partner could come to church with her, but they would not in any way acknowledge them as a couple. And then he told her that if she just repented, she could have "a powerful ministry leading people out of homosexuality."

He didn't know my wife. She turned and walked out, refusing to deny who God created her to be.

Understandably, Heidi spent the next few years wrestling with her faith. More accurately, she wrestled with the church. The evangelical church was obviously not queer affirming, but even the Episcopal Church of her childhood was still working out inclusion in painful ways. It wasn't until she was in her late twenties that she found solid footing in a church again.

Heidi loves God as much as anyone I know. In the end it was God's love for her that called her back into the church. And it was her love for God that helped her to overcome her fear enough to answer the call. Stepping back into a church community after the kind of spiritual abuse she had endured was an act of courageous faith.

I give thanks that my wife found that kind of love. And I feel sad for her college pastor. My sense is that his relationship with God is so fear-based that he couldn't conceive of a God who would dare to love someone like my wife.

Somewhere in the back of his head, in some convoluted way, he cared about my wife enough to think he had to "save her" from hell. But he never stopped to think that maybe by helping her to come out, God was saving her from another kind of hell altogether.

Now my wife is a minister. She spent four years of her ministry on a school campus, where lots of fearful young adults came to her to tell her that they are queer or trans. And Heidi? She looked at them, loved them, and told them "God already knows . . . and God loves you more than you can imagine."

Prayer

God, may your perfect love cast out all my fear, and may my love help others to cast theirs away too.

Chapter 19

YOUR PEOPLE AND MINE

But Ruth said, "Do not press me to leave you or to turn back from following you! Where you go, I will go; where you lodge, I will lodge, your people shall be my people, and your God my God."

—Ruth 1:16

Ever since Fried Green Tomatoes, with its subtly queer subplot, hit theatres in 1991, queer women have loved this verse—a lot. If two women are getting married, I just know that nine times out of ten this is going to be one of the readings.

So when two friends who I was marrying were planning their ceremony with me, I wasn't surprised when they told me they wanted this reading. Then one of them asked me, "So, what's that verse really about? Were they in love?"

"Well," I started, "they were actually mother-in-law and daughter-in-law."

Her face blanched. The biggest challenge of the relationship to date had been getting the mother-in-law-to-be to respect the couple's boundaries. The idea of her going where they would go and lodging where they would lodge was a little too much.

They chose some Indigo Girls' song lyrics instead. Of course they did.

When we marry someone, we marry their family. It doesn't matter if they are their family of origin or their family of choice. Whatever family our spouse chooses to be in relationship with, their people shall be our people, at least on some level.

My wife and I grew up in very different families. She was raised in the north by a single mother—a social worker with a hippie streak. I was raised in the South by my parents, including my father, a career intelligence officer who served in Vietnam. My wife's mom came from a family of seven kids, and family gatherings are loud and boisterous. My own family is smaller and more introverted and formal. When one of her aunts greeted me with a kiss on our first meeting, I didn't know what to do.

Over the years we have learned to love each other's families deeply. But that doesn't mean it didn't take some adjusting on both of our parts. We put in the work, though, because (so long as those relationships are not abusive) to love someone means to at least try to love the people that they love too.

My wife's people are now my people too. And my people are hers. (Truth be told, I think my dad actually likes her more than me.) In the end, that just means that our community of people who love us both is bigger than it's ever been before.

Prayer

God, make me ready to open my heart to new family, and to share my people with my beloved. Amen.

Chapter 20

PLANS

*For surely I know the plans I have for you,
says the LORD, plans for your welfare and not
for harm, to give you a future with hope.*

—Jeremiah 29:11

People love this verse. I see it on social media all the
time, written on notebooks in Instagram-worthy pictures, or quoted in Facebook statuses as a testament
to the kind of wonderful future that the writer thinks
God is preparing for them. And I get it. The idea that
God has something great in store for us is certainly
attractive.

I sometimes wonder, though, has anyone opened
up their Bibles and read the rest of that book? Because
it's not all that reassuring. Jeremiah writes to a community in exile from their homes during the Babylo-
nian captivity. Far from words directed to comfortable
suburban Christians, these are the words of a prophet
to a people longing for a home most of them haven't
seen in decades, if ever. This is hope extended to the
desperate and displaced.

When we grow up queer or trans in a culture
that doesn't fully accept us, it's like being in exile.
We know our true home is out there, even if we can't

quite picture it yet. We long for the day when we can live there as our whole selves, and not as exiles.

God sends hope to the exiled. God tells us that we have a future, and that there is hope. God reassures us that God has plans for us. But God doesn't fix everything in an instant.

The road to home is a long one. For LGBTQ folks, it is often one we have to create for ourselves, carving new pathways in uncharted territory. It can be incredibly exciting and deadly frightening all at once. That is part of what makes LGBTQ people so special. Our very survival depends on our creativity, grit, and integrity.

The good news for us is that God is with us on the journey. God doesn't leave us in exile or forget about us. Instead, God reminds us that we have a true home, one to which God will lead us. Exile will not have the last word. That belongs to God.

Prayer

Dear God, on the days when home seems so far away, remind me that exile is not your will for me. Amen.

Chapter 21

WORTH COMING HOME TO

"You shall love your neighbor as yourself."

—Matthew 22:39

On the morning I decided I couldn't drink anymore, I sat in my car in the parking lot of a local recovery clubhouse, willing myself to go in. I knew that to step into those rooms was to admit something radical, and radically life changing.

I had an Indigo Girls CD in the stereo, and the song "Three County Highway" was playing. The words came out of the speakers and stunned me:

One day I'm coming home to stay, it's true,
And baby, that's the last ticket I'm ever gonna buy.[1]

I knew I needed to do this, but it had been an ultimatum from someone else that got me to the parking lot. I was in a new, promising relationship, and she had said, "Get sober, or I'm gone." Listening to those lyrics, they felt like the promises my heart wanted to make to her.

Jesus teaches that the second part of the greatest commandment is that we should love others as we love ourselves. If you're reading this, you probably already know that you're supposed to love your neighbor. But what so many of us can't wrap our heads around is that Jesus is also telling us that we have to love ourselves. Until we can do that, we aren't going to be any good for anyone else.

I last talked to that woman I thought I'd gotten sober for a year and a half later. I had eighteen months of sobriety under my belt by then. All these years later, I see the relationship more clearly. I see that it wasn't healthy and that she wasn't well. While I'll always have some gratitude to her for giving me the nudge I needed into sobriety, I know now that I didn't get sober for her. I still listen to that song sometimes, but these days it's a little different. I hear that verse and picture it not as my words to her, but as a promise to myself. It was a hope for a better future voiced on one of my lowest days.

Four years after I got sober, I started dating a beautiful woman who sat behind me in class. Today she's my wife and in the home we've built together we do a lot more laughing than crying. I believe that's because before I ever met her, I figured out how to love myself. Before we can ever come home to anyone else, we have to come home to ourselves.

Prayer

God, bring me home to me. I'm worth coming home to. Amen.

Chapter 22

WHEN TO STOP TALKING

All of you are sorry comforters.

—Job 16:2b CEB

When Job lost everything, his friends tried to "help." They came to see him, and for a while they did OK. They kept their mouths shut.

But then they started talking.

Each of the three friends tells Job that he must have sinned somehow. His current afflictions, namely the deaths of all his children, his loss of everything else, and the covering of his body in boils, are God's punishment. But don't worry, they say. Just repent and God will show mercy.

In the 1980s, prominent clergy declared that AIDS was God's punishment for gay men. Sadly, they were not in the minority. Even clergy in what we now think of as progressive denominations would shake their heads and say, "Well, it's a shame, but it's the consequence of living 'that lifestyle.'" Too many people died thinking that God was mad at them enough to kill them.

When you have been told your whole life that something is wrong with you, it's easy to accept that anything bad that happens to you is somehow God's just punishment. But Job refuses to listen to his friends blame him. He tells them that they are really bad at this comforting stuff and reasserts that he does not deserve his suffering. They still don't get it, though. Again and again, they argue that Job must have sinned.

In the epilogue to the story, after God and Job have directly confronted one another, God has a talk with Job's friends. God tells them, "My wrath is kindled against you and against your two friends; for you have not spoken of me what is right" (42:7). In other words, "You lied about who I am and I am angry."

I sometimes wish God would take aside the loud voices that harshly proclaim God's punishment of others. I wish God would directly tell them to stop talking. Sadly, I've yet to see that happen, but I do think God does something else instead.

During the AIDS crisis, a few older ministers I know tried to offer an alternative voice to those who suffered. They'd sit at bedsides and tell the dying that God loved them. They'd preside at the funerals that others would not, and they would comfort the bereaved, saying that God didn't do this to their friend.

There are a lot of "Job's comforters" in the world. But what Job really needed were better friends. People like those older clergy I know, who shared God's love instead of wrath. When our friends are hurting, God is clear which one we're supposed to be.

Prayer

God, help me to offer words that will comfort others. Or at least help me to keep my mouth shut. Amen.

Chapter 23

THE POWER OF WATER

But let justice roll on like a river, righteousness
like a never-failing stream!

—Amos 5:24 NIV

I spend a lot of time just standing around in rivers. Actually, I'm fly fishing, but there's a lot more time spent standing around in the water waiting than there is catching fish. So, I've learned how to get comfortable staying still in a river for extended periods of time.

This is sometimes easier said than done. On my first extended fishing trip, I went back to my cabin after a long morning standing in the icy cold waters of northern New Hampshire. I'd thrown cast after cast upstream, letting the fly work its way downstream. I'd been standing on uneven rocks, with the swift current pushing against one side, and compensating by pushing back into the water with my weight.

I laid down for a nap and drifted off to sleep, only to be awakened by a pain in my upper thigh that was so intense I shot upright. It felt like a charley horse, except about five times worse. No matter what I did—stretching, massage, deep breaths—it wouldn't stop. It took a good ten minutes before the muscles finally calmed down.

That day, I learned the power that water holds. No matter how firmly I think I'm planted in the river's bed, the water just keeps raging. If I hold on tight it might not carry me off, but it won't stop just for me and my comfort.

The prophet Amos calls for justice and righteousness that roar like a mighty river, cutting a path through the lowest valleys of the world. This is the kind of mighty current that carves its way through solid granite and washes away any obstructions.

I've found that when I try to resist the currents of justice, God's call to join in the waters of righteousness, God gives me a wake-up call every bit as urgent as those sharp pains after fishing. It might seem easier to stay standing where I've always stood, or more convenient not to make the journey downstream, but eventually God is going to get my attention.

That's not to say that God punishes us for not being courageous. That's just to say that when God has set something in motion for good, God's not going to let us stand around and miss the boat. God's going to give us just enough of a nudge to get us moving.

Prayer

God, I'm ready to dive in. May I be one more wave in this tide of justice. Amen.

Chapter 24

OVERWHELMED

Do not fear, for I have redeemed you; I have called you by name, you are mine. When you pass through the waters, I will be with you; and through the rivers, they shall not overwhelm you.

—Isaiah 43:1b–2a

I've never been all that steady on my feet. That was my greatest challenge when I took up fly fishing. I would wade out a few steps from the shore, slip on a rock, and wind up neck deep in the river.

Most of the time it was just a matter of picking myself back up, with nothing hurt but my pride. One afternoon, though, I was fishing near a dam that had just released some water. I probed the river with my wading staff and stepped forward into what I thought was solid ground. My foot must have slipped, though, because in an instant I felt myself upended and caught up in a strong current. I reached out my arms to try to grab a rock or tree limb, but the water was too strong. My waders started to fill with water. I panicked and remember thinking to myself, "This is how people drown."

Like many people who have wrestled with their gender identity, I had times early on when I felt like I was drowning. It all felt too big, and I felt like I was trying to stay afloat in dangerous waters. Sometimes I wondered whether I would survive.

Things changed for me when I started to believe that God was with me in the waters, keeping me safe, and swimming along with me. When I finally came to really accept who I was, as a non-binary person whose pronouns were they/their/them, I truly felt that God had brought me through it all. God had called me by name, and I was God's.

In that split second on the river where I wondered if I would make it, my mind somehow went back to a drown-proofing class we all had to take in college: "Don't panic. Don't get overwhelmed. Get to shallower water."

I flipped over onto my back and aimed for the shore. About ten feet later the current pushed me into shallow water. I got my feet back under me. I was safe, and I was alive.

God does not abandon us in the deep waters. Instead, God stays close, and tells us, "Don't be afraid." God leads us away from the rocks, and into the shallow places. Then, when we're ready, God blesses who we are, and sends us back to swim, stronger and more confidently than ever before.

Prayer

When I lose my footing and end up too deep, stay close to me, God. Turn my panic to peace and call me by my name. Amen.

Chapter 25

ASLEEP IN THE STORM

A windstorm arose on the sea, so great that the boat was being swamped by the waves; but [Jesus] was asleep. And [the disciples] went and woke him up, saying, "Lord, save us! We are perishing!"

—Matthew 8:24–25

Every summer I spend a week on Star Island, a retreat center in a cluster of small islands about a ten-mile boat trip from mainland New Hampshire. One year I decided to row across the small Gosport Harbor from Star to Smuttynose Island. I leaned on the oars, and fell into a rhythm, pulling into the cove at Smuttynose about fifteen minutes later.

It was a beautiful sunny day, with blue skies in all directions. But as I was about to land, the island's caretaker came out of his small house with a walkie-talkie in hand, looking distraught. He shouted out, "Turn back! There's a bad storm coming in quickly!"

I looked out to the left and saw it, far off to the west. The blue clouds had turned black and ominous, and we could see lightening flashing below them. It had come seemingly out of nowhere, and now it was coming straight for the islands.

The return trip back across the choppier seas proved harder than before. Suddenly the oars didn't seem to stay in the oar locks quite as easily. The water lapped harder over the edges. The dock seemed farther off. I didn't relax until I was safely on land again, just before a howling storm raged across the island.

I remember thinking about this story while I rowed. Jesus and the disciples were crossing the sea in a boat during a storm, and to the disciples it looked certain that they were about to die. Jesus, on the other hand, was asleep, without a care in the world.

The disciples wake him up, shouting, "We are about to die!" And Jesus, being Jesus, tells the storm to calm down. And it does. And then he has the nerve to say this: "Why were you afraid?"

Really, Jesus?

Sometimes I feel like God is oblivious to the stormy seas we've all been on. So much so that I want to ask Jesus about this story face-to-face one day. Why were they afraid, you asked? How about why were you asleep?

This is one of those rare Scriptures where my hope comes not from God, but from humans. Here it comes from those disciples who dared to call out to God in their hour of greatest fear. They refused to let God incarnate ignore them while they were facing certain destruction.

Sometimes part of our spiritual life as queer and trans folks is daring to call out to God and demand that we live. Sometimes it's the most faithful and holy thing that we can do.

Prayer

God, why are you asleep? Do you not see this storm that rages around me? Even still, I dare to call out to you. Amen.

Chapter 26

SEND ME?

*Then I heard the voice of the Lord saying,
"Whom shall I send, and who will go for
us?" And I said, "Here am I; send me!"*

—Isaiah 6:8

I had no idea why in the world God would call someone like me into ministry. It was the late 1990s and the
idea of a queer minister wasn't exactly popular. Add to
that the fact that my gender wasn't exactly binary, and
I couldn't imagine a person like me ever in the pulpit.

The tug I was feeling toward ministry wouldn't
go away. I went to seminary and set a plan to be a
pastoral care specialist. Queer folks found a greater
welcome in the fields of chaplaincy, pastoral counseling, and teaching than they did in parish ministry.

My second year, I took a preaching class. Much to
my surprise, I loved preaching. To my even greater surprise, it turns out I wasn't bad at it. After a few sermons,
my preaching professor told me that God had given
me a gift, and I needed to use my gift. I responded by
promptly sabotaging myself by preaching a sermon I
knew wasn't good. I'd never be able to pastor a congregation anyway, I reasoned. Why get my hopes up?

I did become a chaplain after my seminary gradu-
ation, and later a graduate student studying pastoral

counseling. And it was fine. It was meaningful ministry. But for me, it lacked any sense of joy. I had the feeling that was because I wasn't using the gifts God had given to me.

When God gives out gifts, God knows exactly who God wants to have them. It's not an accident. Our gifts shouldn't feel like albatrosses around our necks, dragging us down with the weight of unuse. They should be joys, lifting us up and lifting up those whom we serve.

Queer and trans folks are often taught to doubt our gifts. Too often the church has said, "You must be mistaken . . . God wouldn't call someone like you to do something like this." But no one knows the gifts we have been given better than we ourselves do.

I had been ordained more than eight years before I became a parish pastor. When I finally was standing in the pulpit every Sunday, it became clear what God had intended for me to do. It felt like God had been calling for years, and I had been hiding, saying "send someone else."

It could be that you've been hiding too. Maybe you've suspected that God has given you a gift that you have no idea how to use. Don't be scared of it. Instead, unwrap that gift. Learn how to use it. And then, don't stop until you find the place that's ready to let you use it every day. There's a place out there that needs you and your gifts. Here you are. God sends you.

Prayer

God, thank you for my gifts. May I never leave them unopened and unused. Amen.

Chapter 27

AN HONEST WELCOME

"Let your word be 'Yes, Yes' or 'No, No'; anything
more than this comes from the evil one."

—Matthew 5:37

When I was a pastor in Vermont, a new church
plant came to town. It was the sort of place where
the preacher wore jeans and T-shirts, and the music
was led by a rock band. Their motto was "church for
people who hate church." It wasn't really my kind
of place, but that's OK. Everyone deserves a church
where they feel comfortable.

When some younger, non-churchgoing folks I
knew started going to services there, I got curious. I
researched the church planter's backstory and found
that they had been sent to the "mission field" of New
England by a conservative Southern Baptist congregation in Georgia. Then I found a blog they wrote for
folks back home and realized that their theology was
very different from the open-minded, all-are-welcome
vibe they shared on Sundays. Among their beliefs was
that same-sex marriage was sinful, men alone could
be church leaders and teachers, and non-Christians
were damned.

When I told my friends who were attending this
church what the pastors really believed, they looked

at me like I was out of my mind. "They don't believe that," they said. "They love everyone. I'm sure you're misunderstanding." But, like most LGBTQ folks, I've learned to listen when someone tells me what they think of me.

My problem wasn't so much with their beliefs. They're entitled to those. My problem was that they were hiding them from the people who walked through their doors. I imagined a young queer couple who went there, thinking they were loved and affirmed, who might only realize they were not when they asked to be married there. Or a woman who had struggled to find her voice her whole life, who would then be told she couldn't speak from the pulpit. I thought about the pain that would come to folks when they found the truth.

Jesus told his disciples that they should let their "yes" mean "yes" and their "no" mean "no." Coy equivocation doesn't work. Transparency and honesty are what Christ expects, especially when we are dealing with others. Anything less is a form of spiritual manipulation at best, and abuse at worst.

If you are in a community that is not explicit about its welcome of you, it is OK to ask. If the answer is anything less than a full-throated "yes," then the truth is that it's a "no." A church that won't fully welcome you doesn't deserve you. And a church that won't even be honest about that doesn't deserve anyone.

Prayer

When I search for a community to welcome me in, oh God, don't allow me to settle for anything other than a yes that means yes. Amen.

Chapter 28

BEYOND DNA

*"[A]nd Jacob the father of Joseph the husband of Mary,
of whom Jesus was born, who is called the Messiah."*

—Matthew 1:16

A few years ago, a friend tried to get me to join the Daughters of the American Revolution. From the start, there was an issue: I'm not really a "daughter" of anything, so the gendered aspect was off-putting. As I researched further, though, I realized there was another reason I'd never do it.

The DAR wants proof that you are a biological descendant of someone who participated in the American Revolution. I can give them that. My mom's ancestors are brimming with patriots. They are also explicit about something else, though; if you are adopted, you cannot join.

I'm not sure why blood matters so much to them, but it does. The same family could have two kids, one biological and one adopted, and they'd tell that adopted kid, loved by the same descendants of that patriot, that they don't count. The idea disgusted me so much that I gave the DAR no further thought. My father is an adoptee, and if my wife and I have children I will not be the biological parent. How could I be a part of a group that one day wouldn't accept my own kids?

Besides, I reasoned, how many of those members were so sure that their biological great-great-great-grandfathers were really the people their birth certificates said?

The first chapter of Matthew's Gospel gives a long genealogy of Jesus. It was imperative to prove that Jesus was descended from David, the king of Israel, because it was always said that the Messiah would come from his lineage. And right there, twenty-eight generations back, is David.

But here's the interesting part; Jesus is descended from David not on his mother Mary's side, but through his father Joseph. No matter what you think personally of the virgin birth, Matthew's Gospel argues for it in the next chapter. That means that the Gospel tells us that Joseph is not Jesus's biological father, but he's Jesus's father nonetheless, so much so that Jesus's claim to the messianic title comes through him.

It probably wouldn't have been good enough for the "Sons of King David" application, but it was good enough for God.

So often in the queer and trans communities are families that are made complete through adoption. It's a kind of family that not everyone really gets, or respects. And yet Jesus, an adoptee himself, teaches us that it's our love, and not our blood, that gives us our claims to family. Whatever your family looks like, however it was created, it's not just good enough. Indeed, it's exactly how God intended it.

Prayer

God, you create families and give us stories that span generations. Thank you for those who love me, and those I love, no matter what our DNA says. Amen.

Chapter 29

A TRUE FRIEND

*Some friends play at friendship but a true
friend sticks closer than one's nearest kin.*

—Proverbs 18:24

I'm fortunate enough to have some really good
friends. Some I've known for over twenty years, and
others for just a few. Some are friends with both my
wife and I equally, the kind we go to dinner with on
double dates, while others are more friends that I hang
out with one-on-one. Some are the kinds of guys who
will good-naturedly tease me mercilessly, while others are the ones who will put an arm around me and
ask, "How are you really doing, buddy?" (And some,
blessedly, are both.)

I want my friends to know that if they have a flat
tire on the side of the highway at three in the morning, they can call me and I'll come fix it. I have also
learned, though, that I have to let them take care of
me. That part is harder.

About ten years ago, I was living on Cape Cod. I
was flying to my parents' house for Christmas, and so
I caught a quick flight from Provincetown to Boston,
then was supposed to connect to a flight to Virginia.
When we landed in Boston, a snowstorm hit. All
flights out were canceled, and the airport shut down.

I was stranded, for at least the night, unable to get to Virginia and unable to get home.

I resigned myself to sleeping at the airport that night. During a text conversation, I mentioned what had happened to a friend of mine, an older guy who was prone to shaking his head at the jams I got myself in. He lived about two hours away in western Massachusetts. Before I knew it, he was barreling down the Mass Turnpike, scooping me up at Logan and driving me back to his place in the snow. He fed me a good meal, put me to bed in his guest room, and got me on the plane when it flew out the next day.

My buddy didn't "play at friendship." He saw a friend in need, and he knew he could help, so he did it. He was the big brother I didn't know I needed in that moment.

I believe God gives us friendships like this. We need people who are neither spouse nor kin in our circle. People who choose the intimacy of true friendship, not because they are in any way formally bound to do so, but because they like us. And in them, we see just one more aspect of God's love for us.

Prayer

God, thank you for my friends. May I be a good friend to them, and may I let them be a friend to me. Amen.

Chapter 30

FINDING THE WORDS

In the beginning was the Word, and the Word was with God, and the Word was God.

—John 1:1

I was recently talking to my mentor about gender. I've known her since I was twenty years old, and back when we met, there were certainly trans folks (there always have been) but gender identity wasn't talked about as much. (We thought full inclusion meant adding "bisexual" to the phrase "gay and lesbian.") Even in the queer community, trans folks were misunderstood. Non-binary identity was unheard of.

On this recent day, we were talking about what I'd been like in my twenties, about how much I'd struggled with gender but had not been able to explain it. I literally didn't know where to start back then.

"We didn't know the words for it yet," she said gently.

In John's Gospel, Jesus is called the "Word." As a writer, I've always liked that. Words carry tremendous power and depth. They create meaning and make real what we struggle to name.

I sometimes hear people say, "I don't like labels . . . I wish people didn't label themselves so much. Just be you." And, if that works for you personally, that's fine. But for people like me, finding the words to put around what I knew about myself was powerful. It meant that what was inside of me was real.

There is power in naming. When I was able to finally say "I'm non-binary," it was a revelation. All the turmoil, all the having to fit into the male and female boxes, was resolved. I was able to name my reality, and to share it with those I loved.

When people began to really see me for who I was, as a non-binary person, I felt transformed too. It was like the words inside of me had finally been embodied. For maybe the first time in my life, I felt comfortable in my own skin.

John's Gospel tells us that the Word of God became "incarnate" in Jesus Christ. That means that God's Word literally became human. Jesus is supposed to be our example of how to live in this world. I don't think it's any coincidence that God transformed the Word from something we couldn't quite see or imagine into something solid.

Prayer

God, your Word incarnate is my example. May I find the words that incarnate my reality as well. Amen.

Chapter 31

IRON

*Iron sharpens iron, and one person
sharpens the wits of another.*

—Proverbs 27:17

In conservative Christian culture, this text gets a lot of mileage when talking about becoming a man. It's sometimes even written as "one man sharpens another." In that context it is read as a celebration of a certain kind of masculinity, one that is hard and unyielding. That makes me laugh, because the best example in my life of iron sharpening iron comes from a woman I know.

My mentor is more traditionally feminine; gentle and gracious, and petite. I, on the other hand, am masculine and physically imposing. We have a generation's worth of age between us. Put side by side, we are quite different.

And yet, she's been the iron who has sharpened my iron. That's because strength, fortitude, and accountability don't fit into the gender stereotypes we have been taught to believe they should inhabit. She's taught me that a woman, or any feminine person, can be a rock-solid leader and fierce protector.

Looking back, it's interesting to see how she has helped me to become "they." Her transcendence of the traditional gender norms I had come to expect helped me to understand that I was free to do my own exploration. Ironically, this feminine person helped me to become the masculine person I am today.

One of the gifts of the LGBTQ community is that we are queering gender in powerful ways. Because our relationships subvert the traditional male/female binary, we have been given permission to claim roles and traits that we were raised to think were not ours. In fact, sometimes we have had to claim them out of necessity.

Unlike conservative Christianity, this means that we can be open to learning the lessons that form us from people of all genders. Men don't have to mentor other men. Women don't have to just teach other women. And non-binary folks? Well, not only do we get to exist and be seen, but we get to become teachers too, with lessons to teach men, women, and other non-binary folks.

There is nothing wrong with being masculine or feminine or something else entirely. Gender is beautiful when expressed with authenticity. I believe our true gender is a gift from God. It's only when restrictive ideas are imposed of what those genders mean that things get toxic. When we see positive traits in people of all genders, we learn a little more about how to cultivate them in ourselves. In fact, we become more ourselves.

Prayer

God, help me to see the richness of gender in others, and open my heart to the lessons people of every gender have to teach me. Amen.

Chapter 32

AN OPEN DOOR

"Look, I have set before you an open door,
which no one is able to shut."

—Revelation 3:8a

I'm the sort who was never good at picking up when someone was flirting with me. My wife had seen me date other women before her, and always rolled her eyes at me and told me I didn't understand how much they liked me. I shrugged it off and told her she was wrong. Looking back now, I wonder if I knew that I was waiting for her.

My first date with my wife (though I'm so dense that I didn't realize it was a date at the time) was to her church. She wanted me to check out a midweek worship service she loved. So, we met downtown, under the front doors of the building that had this verse carved above them: "Behold, I have set before thee an open door" (KJV).

Somehow, I finally realized she was interested in me, and we started to date. A year later we walked through those same doors, and under those same words, into an empty sanctuary. Kneeling in the aisle, I asked her to walk through the next set of open doors with me and be my wife. A year after that, we walked back under those words and up to the front of the church, where we vowed to love one another our whole lives long.

Some folks pick up on invitations into the lives of others fairly easily. For some of us, though, the big opportunities in our lives should come with big carved signs over them saying "Look! It's an open door!"

Those of us in the LGBTQ community too often rule ourselves out. We don't think that anyone is going to want what we have. We're too queer. Too trans. Too different.

What we don't realize is that there's someone out there who is looking for us. Someone who is going to see us for exactly who we are and say, "You are what I've been waiting for . . . come on in." We don't have to settle for someone who could possibly love us. We get to wait until the right door is open and we are being enthusiastically invited in.

I think God sees us like that too. I think God sees us in all our queer and trans glory and thinks, "You! I've been waiting for you!" I think God opens wide the doors to God's heart, and tells us, "Get in here—I've been waiting for you. What do you need? A sign carved in stone?"

If you're like me, yeah, probably so. The good news is that it's there. God carved it right onto you when God created you in God's image. And you are good. The open door is within yourself, and God is waiting to welcome you home.

Prayer

God, before I can even knock, throw open the door and welcome me in. Amen.

Chapter 33

BUILT TO LAST

"Everyone then who hears these words of mine and acts on them will be like a wise man who built his house on rock. The rain fell, the floods came, and the winds blew and beat on that house, but it did not fall, because it had been founded on rock."

—Matthew 7:24–25

As children we learn the story of the three little pigs. One built a house out of straw, another of sticks, and the third of bricks. We're taught that when the big bad wolf came, he was able to blow the first two houses down easily, but the brick house stood strong.

When we grow up in, or are even just exposed to, the ideas of a religious tradition that teaches a shallow theology around gender and sexuality, it is like our houses have been built of straw and sticks. When we are faced with the complexities of sexuality and gender, our old ideas fall apart, and sometimes the entire house of our faith falls down.

There are two ways to see this. One is as a tragedy. We've learned that the worldview we had around something important was wrong, so that means our entire faith must be counterfeit as well. But the other is to see it as an opportunity. When a house that was never all that stable falls apart, it's as good a time as ever to rebuild with something stronger.

Jesus talks about the wise man who builds his house on rock instead of sand. When the big bad wolf of storms and floods comes, they cannot touch him.

To live in a homophobic and transphobic society, no matter what our own faith development was like, means that at least part of our house was built on sand. To dare to rebuild a more mature faith, one that rejects the negative messaging of fear, is to rebuild that part of our house on rock solid ground. The wind and the rains will always come. There are a lot of big bad wolves out there. But a well-built house will always stand. Sitting inside, with the ones you love, you can look out the windows and laugh at the storms.

Prayer

God, when my house feels shaky, blow it down. And then, help me to build again—this time to last. Amen.

Chapter 34

PANICKED FAITH

Cast all your anxiety on God,
because God cares for you.

—1 Peter 5:7

The first time I had a panic attack, it was terrifying. My heart raced, my breathing shallowed and quickened, my hands grew clammy, and my mind raced. I thought I might be having a heart attack.

An ER visit and EKG later, the doctor assured me I was not. Instead, I was a newly sober graduate student under a lot of pressure and without my preferred method of self-medicating. For the first time in a while, I was having to deal with my fears and anxieties directly.

I felt deeply ashamed of my anxiety. Didn't Scripture tell me not to worry? Surely if I just had a little more faith, I would know in my heart that God would make everything OK. Friends would tell me that I just had to trust more, pray more, believe more.

They meant well, but they were talking about the everyday worry that all of us have. They weren't talking about the kind of anxiety that can literally take our breath away. That kind of anxiety is a legitimate and physical thing. Our body manifests what is happening chemically in our brain, and it can be terrifying.

So is there no hope for the anxious among us? No. First, there are ways to get better. Therapy, medication, and good coping strategies all matter.

But there's also the spiritual component. I no longer believe God is disappointed in us for being anxious. Instead, I think God understands that our anxiety is a natural reaction to a very broken world.

The author of First Peter doesn't tell us to stop being anxious. Instead, the author says, "Cast all your anxiety on God, because God cares for you." Put another way, God loves you so much and wants to be with you when you are feeling anxious.

In the moments when it feels like the world is crashing down, the last thing we need is to think God can't handle our pain. God isn't angry at you for your anxiety. God is scooping you up, holding you tight, and sitting with you through the worst of it.

Prayer

Sometimes I am so afraid, God, that my whole body feels it. Stay close to me. Amen.

Chapter 35

LOVE AND WORK

"Come to me, all you who are struggling hard and carrying heavy loads, and I will give you rest. Put on my yoke, and learn from me. I'm gentle and humble. And you will find rest for yourselves. My yoke is easy to bear, and my burden is light."

—Matthew 11:28–30 CEB

Clergy are known workaholics even within a greater culture that celebrates workaholism. A friend of mine, though, takes the cake. She is constantly working and has been for decades. Now, nearing retirement age, she shows no sign of slowing down.

She doesn't complain, but I can see the toll it's taking. She looks more tired every time I see her. Her affect seems flat. Her days seem like twelve-hour-long grinds without any break. I know she likes what she does, but I worry that there is little real joy for her at work anymore.

When I read this particular translation of Jesus' words, I was struck by it. "I'm gentle and humble," says Jesus. "My yoke is easy to bear, and my burden is light."

Somewhere along the line, too many of us conflated God with a taskmaster boss. Even if we preach a gospel of grace and forgiveness, we hold ourselves to draconian standards when it comes to our productivity. Somewhere, in the back of our minds, we think God is hovering, waiting to give us our next performance review.

Our work is important, paid and unpaid. It gives us meaning and purpose. It should challenge us. But it shouldn't break us.

I think that many of us who are queer and trans picked up on the fact that we would have to work a lot harder than others to be seen as competent. It's a lesson I know my friend internalized well. No one doubts how good she is at what she does.

Still, I worry that when my friend finally does retire, she will lose her sense of self-worth. When she isn't the one who must respond to the crisis or lead the meeting or fix the problem, who will she be?

There are days when I want to take the heavy yoke she has pulled for too long off her shoulders. I want her to feel what it's like to live without that pressure. I want her to believe that, far from our harsh supervisor, God is our partner in this work. And sometimes trusting God means trusting that you can take a break, and let God take over for a bit.

Prayer

God, may I never conflate too completely my love for you and my work for you. Amen.

Chapter 36

CONQUERED

"I have said this to you, so that in me you may have peace. In the world you face persecution. But take courage; I have conquered the world!"

—John 16:33

Jesus was trying to prepare his disciples for what they would face for following him. It would be a hard road, full of judgment and isolation. They would face the world's persecution. They would suffer, literally, for the gospel. And yet, said Jesus, there was reason to take heart. The same world that would persecute them, that would make their lives miserable, had already been "conquered" by Jesus.

If I were a disciple, I'd have some questions. First, if the world had been conquered by Jesus, why was he still allowing it to torment those who loved him? Conversely, was the fact that they were still being tormented a sign that maybe Jesus had not, in fact, conquered the world? Did Jesus even know what he was talking about?

When you go back to the original Greek text, the word translated here as "conquered" has a different meaning: "overcome." It's less the image of the conquering hero, and more the description of one who has struggled through the morass and made it to the other side.

Things have changed rapidly in recent decades. To be openly LGBTQ is, in many ways, easier than it used to be. But we are still people who are subject to persecution. Each of us will face bigotry and discrimination that we would not face were we straight or cisgender.

It is that part of me that identifies with the "overcoming Jesus" more than the "conquering Jesus." I take comfort in the idea that God incarnate struggled along the hardest paths and emerged on the other side. Jesus knows what it is to face the worst the world can do.

The good news is this: Nothing in the world, not even the grave, could destroy Jesus. And, Christ tells us, it cannot destroy us either.

Does it make the moments of injustice any less painful? Maybe not. But it does give me a peace that I would not have without my faith. We follow a Savior who dares to slug through the trenches with us, one who has already made this trip before, and one who will lead us safely to the other side.

Prayer

Jesus, when I am hemmed in by the world, liberate me. You know the way out. Amen.

Chapter 37

PULLED BACK

*Even though I walk through the darkest
valley, I fear no evil; for you are with me; your
rod and your staff—they comfort me.*

—Psalm 23:4

Someone once explained the "rod and staff" of Psalm 23 to me like this: God guides us with the staff, and beats us with the rod, and we should be grateful for both because God only punishes the ones God loves. That didn't sit well with me.

David, the one given credit for writing this Psalm, was a shepherd in his childhood. He knew the tools of his trade. So, when David writes about God as a shepherd, he would have chosen his words carefully.

It turns out that neither rod nor staff were ever used to hit the sheep. The staff was indeed used to guide them, and to gently keep them moving in the right direction. It was a way to create a path.

The rod, on the other hand, was used when things got hard. When a sheep got stuck, fell into deep waters, or got a little too far away, the crooked handle of the rod would be used to gently pull them out of danger. In a pinch, if anyone tried to attack the sheep, the rod could even be used to fend them off.

I don't know why some have tried to reinterpret a beautiful metaphor of God's protection into one of a God who punishes us, but I suspect that it's because we are uncomfortable with being loved by a tender, forgiving God who is the first to come to our aid when we are in trouble. We understand better the angry parent who hurts us "for our own good."

But that's not who God is.

A gay man I once knew saw the bad things that happened to him as God's punishment for homosexuality. I assured him that was not true, but I wish I'd had better understanding of this image at the time. God wasn't beating him. Instead, God was running after him, ready to pull him out of harm's way, and ready to defend him against predators. Why? Because that's what good shepherds do.

Prayer

God, your rod and your staff, they comfort me. Guide me always, and rescue me when I wander off. Amen.

Chapter 38

LAID OPEN

"No one has greater love than this, to lay
down one's life for one's friends."

—John 15:13

I never hid the fact that I was non-binary in my gender from my congregation. At the same time, I never pressed the issue. If people used my correct pronouns (they/them/their), I appreciated it, but if people defaulted to feminine pronouns, I didn't correct them.

That changed when one of our youth came out as trans. As he began his transition, I realized that he was watching me be misgendered regularly. By my not saying anything, I was teaching him that it was OK for others to not respect your gender.

I told his parents that I was going to talk about why pronouns were important in a sermon, and that I was going to talk explicitly about my own gender identity. I wanted their son to be able to choose whether or not to be there that day, as it would likely hit close to home.

On the morning of the sermon, I was nervous. I stood in the narthex waiting for the prelude to begin. How would people react? Was there a chance I'd be run out of town? I just kept thinking about that young man in my church and thinking about this verse. I reassured myself that no matter what happened to me, even if I lost my position, I was doing the right thing because it would make his life easier.

Just then that young man, the one I'd been so worried about, bounced up the stairs and put his arm around me.

"You've got this," he said. "You're going to do great."

He was right. Things were great. The congregation, much to my embarrassment, responded with a prolonged ovation when I finished preaching. I heard positive feedback, and in the coming weeks extra effort was made by all to use my correct pronouns. And none of that mattered half as much as the reaction of that young man, who hugged me after the service while I told him that he would always be seen at our church.

At the end of the day, I realized that I hadn't been the one to be brave in that moment. I wasn't sacrificing for him, or any other trans youth. Instead, he was teaching me, by the way he was living his own life at age fourteen, what it means to be yourself in the world. He taught me that I needed to be able to say that I, too, would always be seen at our church. He wouldn't let me settle for anything less.

Prayer

God, may we learn from our friends of all ages, who are laying open their lives for us. Amen.

Chapter 39

BELIEVED

*"Which of you convicts me of sin? If I tell
the truth, why do you not believe me?"*

—John 8:46

One of the most disheartening things that can happen
to someone who is newly out about being queer or
trans is not being believed. "Oh, it's just a phase," says
a parent. Or, "They're just doing it to get attention,"
says a classmate. "Just give it time . . . they'll change."

Certainly, our understandings of the nuances of
our identities do change. Maybe a trans man first
came out as a lesbian, and only later began to understand their gender identity. Maybe a man who is bi
first said that he was gay. If we are growing, then
through the years we will be revealed to ourselves in
deeper and deeper ways.

But that's different than someone assuming
we are wrong when we tell the truth about who we
understand ourselves to be.

I've never understood the impulse to tell someone they are wrong about themselves. Coming out
publicly is a deeply personal and vulnerable act, one
that has likely created years of internal struggle for
the person doing it. And yet, even in the LGBTQ

community, I've heard members doubting the professed identities of others.

I come back to Jesus' question: "Why do you not believe me?"

I've learned to trust that when others share their stories of who they are, my task is to just listen and be grateful for the gift of their sharing. When they tell me their pronouns, I learn them and use them, even if they are surprising at first. If they share that they are suddenly dating a woman, after years of only being with men, I trust that they know to whom they are attracted far better than I do.

It is never our job to police the identities of others. Instead, our work as faithful people is to say, "I see you, and I'll do my best to make sure others see you too." This is deeply holy work, not just because it makes life easier for those we love, but also because when we affirm the ways that others see themselves, in their particular *imago Dei*, we are able to see for ourselves just another way that God sees God's self too.

Prayer

> *God, may we learn to recognize your complex being and beauty in all whom we meet, and may we trust that it is good. Amen.*

Chapter 40

ENJOYING LIFE

*So I commend enjoyment, for there is nothing
better for people under the sun than to eat,
and drink, and enjoy themselves, for this will
go with them in their toil through the days of
life that God gives them under the sun.*

—Ecclesiastes 8:15

As a newly out college student, I was a very earnest young activist. I saw the pain of our community and wanted to fix it. I protested. I marched. I raged against every slight and insult hurled at us.

I probably wasn't a lot of fun at parties.

Ironically, it wasn't until after I got sober that I started to learn how to enjoy myself. I remember eating a piece of chocolate cake one night, and really tasting and enjoying it for the first time. "Wow," I thought, "this is really good!"

I'm married now to an exceptionally hardworking woman who also very deliberately tries to make time for fun and joy. She's taught me how to do things like take vacations, look forward to nice meals out, and treat myself to the occasional indulgence.

Recently, I found a leather work bag that I had wanted for years on sale in a store. Even at half-price, I was unable to justify the expense to myself. I stood by the display for nearly ten minutes, and texted my wife, telling her about it and telling her why buying it didn't make sense.

Finally, she texted back, "Look, if you don't buy it for yourself, I'm going to call the store and say 'You see the sketchy guy who keeps touching the leather bags? That one's mine. They'll take it.'"

Did I need it? No. But now every morning I pick up that bag on my way to work and think about how it's OK to do something nice for ourselves from time to time. Even when the world is broken. Even when we can't fix it yet.

Am I saying we should all be reckless hedonists or spendthrifts? No. Of course not. But should we find small moments of joy in a world that too often does its best to grind us down? I believe so. If we wait for a perfect world until we let ourselves be happy, we will never have a good day in all our lives. In the end, I don't think that God wants that for any of us.

Prayer

God, today help me to eat, drink, and be merry. And help me to create a world where others can do the same. Amen.

Chapter 41

IMAGO DEI

Then God said, "Let us make humankind in our image, according to our likeness."

—Genesis 1:26a

Every LGBTQ person knows what it's like to be in a place where they are not welcome. Sure, people might tell you that you are, but deep down you know that a welcome like that comes with a big asterisk: "You are welcome here, but only so long as you are trying to change."

A welcome that does not allow us to be our full selves, or that asks us to sacrifice intimacy and love for acceptance, is no welcome at all. But beyond that, it's a request that we hide ourselves, and, in the process, hide the image of God that we possess because it somehow threatens another person's image of God. That's more than mere inhospitality; that's idolatry.

God, of course, transcends gender and sexuality. God is neither male nor female, gay nor straight, cis nor trans, binary nor non-binary. God is simply God.

But if that's true, that means that queer and trans folks are a reminder that God is more expansive than we will ever truly understand. If we are all created in God's image, that means our queer and trans selves are too. There is something in our very being that testifies to the wild and beautiful diversity of God's own being.

When someone rejects that wonderful reality of who you are, they are rejecting the image of God because it challenges the limits on who God can be. Your existence testifies to a God who is bigger than others can imagine. That is an incredibly scary thing. But, just maybe, you can show them that God is more amazing than they even know.

After all, if you blow their mind, can you imagine what God is going to do?

Prayer

God, thank you for making me like you. And thank you for all the ways I see you in others. May your image be recognized and celebrated in us all. Amen.

Chapter 42

DUST-FREE

"If anyone will not welcome you or listen to your words, shake off the dust from your feet as you leave that house or town. Truly I tell you, it will be more tolerable for the land of Sodom and Gomorrah on the day of judgment than for that town."

—Matthew 10:14–15

When I was attending a Presbyterian seminary during the height of the denomination's debates about gay ordination, there were a lot of calls for conversation. "We need to learn to just sit down and talk," a "moderate" voice told us. "This could all be solved if gay folks could listen to exclusive voices," and vice versa.

I'm not going to tell you that relationships aren't key to transformation. They are. But I am going to say this: It is not the obligation of a marginalized person to invest the emotional labor of explaining their worthiness to someone else.

There are some LGBTQ folks who enjoy doing the work of talking with those who believe differently from them. Many more of us, though, do not. The task of sitting with someone who believes that you are lesser, or that you must change, is exhausting. At its worst, it's abusive. And hear this clearly: God does not call us into abuse.

You have every right to walk away from conversations that demean your worth and dignity. It is not your job to convince people to love you. If you are not welcome, and your voice is not heard, you get to shake the dust off your feet and leave.

For those who would be allies, this is your work, not just around LGBTQ concerns, but around any inequality. Those of us who are white need to do the work of dismantling racism and white privilege. Those who are male must confront misogyny. Those who are Christian must stand against anti-Semitism and Islamophobia.

Each of us has some privilege that we can use on behalf of others. And many of us also have some part of ourselves that we need to protect from the harshness of intolerance. When we invest our energy not in debates we cannot win, but rather in relationships with those who will partner in the work with us, we have the power to truly build the coalitions that can change things for the better. For everyone.

Prayer

God, when it's time for me to shake the dust off my feet, give me the confidence of peace. And when it's time for me to speak up for others, give me a voice. Amen.

Chapter 43

FACING DOWN LIONS

*Then [King Darius] gave the command, and Daniel
was brought and thrown into the den of lions. The
king said to Daniel, "May your God, whom you
faithfully serve, deliver you!" . . . Then the king went
to his palace and spent the night fasting; no food
was brought to him, and sleep fled from him.*

—Daniel 6:16, 18

Everyone thinks the most interesting part of the book
of Daniel has to do with Daniel somehow surviving
being thrown into a den of lions. To me, King Darius,
the guy who threw him in there, is the big draw.

Daniel was one of Darius's many lieutenants,
and his favorite one at that. While the king's other
appointed men took bribes, Daniel was above corruption. This threatened the others, and so they hatched
a plot. They got the king to agree to a new law that
demanded that for thirty days no one could pray to
anything or anyone other than the king himself, or
else they would be thrown to the lions.

Daniel was a devout believer and kept praying
to God. After catching Daniel in the act, the plotters
demanded that the king carry out the punishment.
Darius tried to find a loophole but could not. He put

Daniel in the lion's den, and went home wracked with sorrow, because hungry lions usually win.

The question for me is this: He was the king; if he really wanted to save Daniel, who was going to stop him? My guess is that Darius was worried he'd lose face if he didn't carry out the penalty. And so, he chose to sacrifice Daniel rather than show costly moral courage.

Sometimes it's tempting to choose safety when I'm called to be courageous. As a queer person, I've dodged a lot of lions. My life is less scary these days, and I like it that way. So, when I see someone else being led to the lions, it's tempting to just turn away and keep silent, lest I be next.

But my faith tells me no one deserves the lions' den. Others were morally courageous on my behalf, and it's my turn to pass it on. It might not make me popular, but in the end, I'll have a lot fewer sleepless nights—and probably a lot more friends who haven't become lion food.

Prayer

God, when the lions get hungry, don't let me stand by while my friends are thrown to them. Amen.

Chapter 44

BEYOND NEUTRALITY

*Then Herod sent the [magi] to Bethlehem,
saying, "Go and search diligently for the child;
and when you have found him, bring me word
so that I may also go and pay him homage."*

—Matthew 2:8

When corruption gains power, the greatest threat is competition. King Herod understood that. He was ruthless, unjust, and paranoid. So, when three wise folks from other lands showed up at his place, talking about a new king who had just been born in his kingdom, he decided to eliminate the threat.

Bishop Desmond Tutu once said, "If you are neutral in situations of injustice, you have chosen the side of the oppressor. If an elephant has its foot on the tail of a mouse and you say that you are neutral, the mouse will not appreciate your neutrality." In other words, when it comes to justice, no choice is a choice to side with the oppressor.

Herod sent the magi on to find Jesus, telling them to let him know when they did. But, being wise, they figured out his plan. If they shared Jesus' location with Herod, they knew the child would be killed. And so, after they worshiped the baby themselves, they avoided Herod by going home "by another road" (2:12).

Being wise means choosing our loyalties well. The magi could have stayed "neutral" and told Herod where to find Jesus. But they refused to collude with the elephant when there was a mouse who needed protection.

It is sometimes tempting to stay neutral in times of conflict, particularly if we've been those mice who have somehow lived to tell about it. Bishop Tutu reminds us that there's no such thing as moral neutrality. True wisdom is understanding that and asking for the courage to side with the mouse.

Prayer

God, who am I to fear elephants when you are on the side of the smallest creatures? Amen.

Chapter 45

LOVING THE CHILD

"'Lord, when was it that we saw you hungry and gave you food, or thirsty and gave you something to drink? . . . And the king will answer them, 'Truly I tell you, just as you did it to one of the least of these who are members of my family, you did it to me.'"

—Matthew 25:37b, 40

Every Christmas Eve our church sanctuary fills with worshipers. It's a picture-perfect, small town New England evening. We dim the lights, pass the flame from row to row, and the church glows with hundreds of lit candles as we sing "Silent Night."

I tell the congregation that when we blow out those candles, they each can make the choice to carry the light of Christ in their hearts all year long. This past year, though, I offered a caveat: Don't light your candle unless you really intend to take the words of the man this baby would grow up to be seriously.

Jesus taught that what we do to others we do to him. In other words, if you really love the child in the manger at Christmas, then you should love every other child in this world on every other day. In fact, you cannot love this child in the manger if you do not love the others too.

And so, if you love the baby who was born with nothing in a barn, then you should love the children who are born into poverty today. If you love the child who had to flee with his parents to a new land, then you should love the children who are alone without their parents at the border tonight. If you love the child who would become the Prince of Peace, then you should love the children who are scared about violence at their schools. And if you love that baby, you should love every baby who, in the fullness of time, will share that they are LGBTQ. You can't love the baby and hate the adult. Period.

The work of loving this Christ child doesn't end with the last lines of "Silent Night." In fact, that's when it starts. And that work lasts all year long.

Prayer

God, help me to carry your light in my heart, on winter nights, on summer days, and every hour in between. Amen.

Chapter 46

FIVE STARS

*Finally, beloved, whatever is true, whatever is
honorable, whatever is just, whatever is pure,
whatever is pleasing, whatever is commendable,
if there is any excellence and if there is anything
worthy of praise, think about these things.*

—Philippians 4:8

A few years ago, I was browsing some online reviews
on a rating site. It was the sort of site that started a
restaurant review with, "Four stars . . . pretty good,"
or, "One star . . . I got food poisoning."

My personal favorites, though, are natural wonders. Places like the Grand Canyon, which received
this review: "As amazing as the views are, it's really
kind of boring. Every 500 feet a new vantage point of
the same thing: a really big hole in the ground. One
star."

Paul tells the church in Philippi that "if there is
any excellence and if there is anything worthy of
praise, think about these things." Appreciate them.
Recognize them. God gave them to us because they
are worth celebrating.

This world is full of one-star voices. Those are the
people who see the greatest, most wondrous things
and shrug. Some of those people will look at you, in

all of your queer or trans glory, and hit that one-star review.

When they do, remember that there are people out there who hate the Grand Canyon. It's true; there's no accounting for taste, and that means that even you are not immune from the bad reviews of those who have no taste. But that doesn't mean that you're not fabulous.

The same God who made rivers and canyons and big skies made you too. And then, God promptly gave you five stars. No matter what the one-star voices say, that's the only review that matters.

Prayer

God, you have created this world full of wonder and awe, and I'm a part of it. Help me to live into every bit of that fabulousness. Amen.

Chapter 47

A WISER GENERATION

Let no one despise your youth, but set the believers an example in speech and conduct, in love, in faith, in purity.

—1 Timothy 4:12

A fifty-something year old gay man recently was talking about younger LGBTQ folks. He said, "You know, they only use the word 'queer' because they want attention. I guess being 'gay' isn't good enough for them anymore."

A few of us pushed back, explaining that "queer" was seen by some as more inclusive because it better included the nuances of gender and sexual attraction than "gay" or "lesbian" or even "bisexual." He wasn't hearing it. To him it was just another example of how "kids today" shouldn't be taken seriously.

The blessing of an intergenerational community is that we learn from one another. Yes, our elders bring us a history we need to know and learn. Their struggle created our paths to freedom. They should never be taken for granted. But those kids we are so quick to dismiss? They've got some answers too.

I don't think that being younger always makes you right, but I do think that young people bring new and important ways of understanding the world to those of us who are middle-aged or older. To see the world with new eyes, and to make meaning of it, is to create new paradigms that could free us all.

Nearly every time I talk with the youth of my church about a Bible story, they show me a new way of looking at it, some nuance I've overlooked. They make the faith fresh and inspire my belief. When I sit down with LGBTQ youth, they do the same. Far from being the older person who shows up with all the answers, I've learned from them new ways to understand gender and orientation that have liberated me.

Years from now, today's youth will be the elders. Maybe the job of those of us who are elders or near-elders now is to teach them by example how to be the elders we hope they will one day be by listening, by learning, and by taking them seriously. Whether in church, or the queer community, it's not a bad practice to embrace.

Prayer

God, you keep transforming us, and sometimes we are not your messengers. Help us to hear the promises that are being given to us, no matter the age of the bearer. Amen.

Chapter 48

APPROVED BY GOD

*Am I now seeking human approval,
or God's approval? Or am I trying to please
people? If I were still pleasing people,
I would not be a servant of Christ.*

—Galatians 1:10

I love wearing bow ties. I have a big collection, full of different colors and patterns, hanging on the back of my closet door.

I'd wear them sometimes, but never to work. On Sundays I'd get dressed for church, in khakis and collared shirts, thinking about how I'd like to wear one to worship. For years, I didn't. I presented in a masculine style, but I wondered if the bow tie would be a step too far for some. My congregation embraced their gender nonconforming pastor enough—would this be pushing too hard?

And then, one Sunday, I did it. I tied on a blue tie with small stars and went to church. I walked into the sanctuary, up to the deacons who were setting up, and braced myself. One looked at me casually, said "I like your tie," and went back to what he was doing.

The whole morning was like that. I preached in a bow tie, and somehow the whole church didn't come crashing down. When I confided in another queer parishioner that it was my first time wearing a tie at church, they looked confused and said, "Really? I thought you always did?"

I had spent so much mental energy on those bow ties. It made me wonder how much time I'd spent trying to seek approval from others, instead of just joyfully being the person God had created me to be.

Now, every time I wonder if I should edit my queerness or transness in some way to please others, I just look at that rack of bow ties, and realize I'm overthinking things. The funny thing is, I think I've become a better pastor and preacher ever since. I'm not hiding any part of myself in the pulpit anymore. I'm fully me, and that shines through. People see it, and trust it, and can relate.

These days, I wear a bow tie every Sunday. Aside from the occasional compliment (and a few gifted ties), the only problem I have now is that I need a second tie rack.

Prayer

Dear God, may I never be less than who you have created me to be out of fear that I may displease others. Amen.

Chapter 49

STRONG AND TENDER

I am distressed for you, my brother Jonathan;
greatly beloved were you to me; your love to me
was wonderful, passing the love of women.

—2 Samuel 1:26

I've often heard that David and Jonathan were gay. How else can you explain the line about David loving him more than women? And, perhaps, they were. We don't know the workings of their hearts and minds.

What's more interesting to me about this text is the idea of two men deeply loving one another, whether romantic or not. Too often we are taught that deep love is not a masculine virtue, especially when exhibited between two masculine individuals.

I once was talking to a friend of mine who is a self-identified butch. I asked her if she had ever found herself attracted to other butches or to transmasculine individuals. She looked at me sideways. "No," she said. "That's just unnatural."

I was struck by her use of the word "unnatural." Despite being raised as a girl, she had internalized the message that so many boys are taught at a young age: you cannot show affection to one another. It's unnatural.

There is nothing wrong with masculinity. It's toxic masculinity, a corruption and betrayal of what is good about masculinity, that's the problem. The idea that to show gentleness, affection, or love is somehow weakness has contributed to so much violence and fear.

Scripture shows us that two men, strong and decisive, capable of leading armies, loved each other deeply and without fear. No matter their attraction to one another, that is a queer story because it turns gender expectations on its head. At the end of the day, transcending those false limits of affection will save more than just LGBTQ people. It could save us all.

Prayer

God, the love you give to us for one another is wonderful. May I never let it be defined by my fears. Amen.

Chapter 50

HALF AS HARD

Two are better than one, because they have a
good reward for their toil. For if they fall, one
will lift up the other; but woe to one who is alone
and falls and does not have another to help.

—Ecclesiastes 4:9–10

About a month into dating my now-wife, Heidi, I got really sick. I had a virus that made my temperature shoot up to 103 degrees. I drifted in and out of consciousness, coming to and finding her looking at me with concern. She brought me medicine, soup, and tea. Far from being comforted, I got defensive.

"I'm fine," I told her. "I've been able to keep myself alive for 34 years. I don't need help."

"OK," she said. "But maybe you don't need to do it all by yourself anymore."

Since that day, we've both taken care of one another. I confess that it is still easier for me to give help than to receive it, but I've gotten a little better at it. (Even though I still lovingly refer to Heidi as "the warden" when I'm sick.)

My wife has a saying about our marriage: "Twice as good. Half as hard." She's right. Heidi makes every day a little better and a little easier. But this isn't an advertisement for marriage. You don't have to marry someone to accept care from them. Instead, it's a reminder that community matters, and that vulnerability is sometimes a way of showing your community that you love and trust them enough to need them.

Too often I hear about a queer or trans person suffering alone because they don't want to burden others. I think loneliness is one of the most lethal afflictions of our community. The irony is that we are a community of helpers and healers. Most of us genuinely want to be allowed to care.

Our faith revolves around a God who was vulnerable enough to become human, and to depend on others. By example, God shows us what it is to be loved by community. On the days when I get stubbornly independent, I remember that even Jesus genuinely needed his friends. And then I pick up the phone and dare to accept help.

Prayer

God, when isolation is more attractive than community, help me to know that's when I need others the most. Amen.

Chapter 51

SURPRISING SAINTS

*Therefore encourage one another and build
up each other, as indeed you are doing."*

—1 Thessalonians 5:11

My friend Devioune was one of the last of a dying
breed. She was an old-school butch dyke who had been
rounded up in bar raids and roughed up by homophobic cops. She ran her business, an erotica boutique,
wearing a leather vest with her pet bulldog by her side.

She didn't know what to make of me when we
first met. I was a Southern expat in New England
with a seminary degree. She was a Jewish New England native who detested the homophobia of the loud
Christian churches who had cheered while her friends
died of AIDS.

Somehow the naive young preacher and the
world-weary purveyor of sex toys became fast friends.

Dev also became one of my biggest cheerleaders.
When I grew frustrated in my search for a first church
to pastor, she would encourage me to keep submitting
applications and writing sermons. When I went on
bad first dates, she would laugh and give me advice.
When I met my now-wife, she rejoiced.

A few years ago, I missed a call from Dev.
Swamped, I texted her and told her I'd call her back

in the next few days. Then, one morning I went on Facebook and saw tribute after tribute being posted about her. She had collapsed and died unexpectedly.

I still miss her. Every All Saints' Day, I pray for her. I'm not sure how she'd feel about that, first because of our faith difference, but mostly because of the "saint" part.

The truth of the matter, though, is that Dev probably did as much to encourage me to become a pastor as any Christian I knew at the time. She built me up when my confidence had been crushed. To me, she was a saint.

In her old store, her leather vest now hangs framed on the wall. People remember and share stories. It turns out there were a lot of us that were encouraged and built up by Dev.

When I die, I hope she and that bulldog meet me in the next life. Then maybe I can tell her what she did. Maybe we all can.

Prayer

God, thank you for the saints who love us into being. Especially for the surprising ones. Amen.

Chapter 52

NONCONFORMED

*Do not be conformed to this world, but be
transformed by the renewing of your minds, so
that you may discern what is the will of God—
what is good and acceptable and perfect.*

—Romans 12:2

We all struggle with wanting to conform. Even the
most vocal of the nonconformists among us do. The
world around us tells us what is expected and acceptable, and we either fall in line, or find a way to stand
out that is still not too far a deviation from the norm.

In high school, I was on the speech and debate
team. We were expected to dress up for competitions.
I envied the boys who could put on a navy blazer with
khakis and a tie. It was the early 1990s, and I struggled with finding a look that wouldn't rattle the judges
but would still let me feel like I wasn't dressing up in
a female-presenting costume.

My coach pulled me aside one day and gave me
some advice on how to do better in tournaments.
Her final line was this: "You are a young lady. Dress
like one."

I was fifteen and her words cut me to the core. I
had reached the point where I was doing well at these
competitions, but she was clear with me that I would

never do any better if I didn't learn to conform to the gendered expectations of dressing up. Beyond that, I knew that I was anything but a "young lady."

Years later my go-to outfit on Sunday mornings is a navy blazer, khakis, and a tie. I'm sure visitors to the church I serve are sometimes confused by that. I've heard them refer to me as "he" before the service starts, only to hear me introduce myself as "Emily." When I get behind the pulpit, though, I'm now able to preach with a confidence and self-acceptance that fifteen-year-old me never had.

Conformity is easy. Allowing your mind to be transformed and renewed is not. You will have days when you feel like a fish out of water, gasping for air while those around you sail through life. I remain convinced, though, that when we can express our true selves, whether through name or gender or dress, we glorify a God who is bigger than the rules of this world. We become as "good and acceptable and perfect" as we can hope to be.

Prayer

God, when conformity looks easy, help me to hold up a mirror, and to find the me you created me to be. Amen.

Chapter 53

GOD BESIDE US

And I heard a loud voice from the throne saying,
"See, the home of God is among mortals.
God will dwell with them;
they will be God's peoples,
and God will be with them;
God will wipe every tear from their eyes.
Death will be no more;
mourning and crying and pain will be no more,
for the first things have passed away."

—Revelation 21:3–4

The text came in over the pager. A man had been admitted to the emergency room. He had AIDS and had collapsed. Not long after being admitted, he lost consciousness. It didn't look good. Could a chaplain come down and sit with his friend who was distraught?

It was the summer of 1999, and the Midtown Atlanta hospital was located in a gay-friendly neighborhood. Even the most willfully ignorant hospital employee would have known that the man crying in the waiting room was the patient's partner. Yet when he tried to access his partner's bedside, the charge nurse rebuked him: "You're not family."

He was, of course. Before long, compassionate nurses brought him back to see his partner, and he remained by his side for the next few days, faithful to the end. Over twenty years on, I still remember the way he cried out when the doctor finally pronounced his beloved's death. In that terrible cry was all the evidence anyone would have needed to know that they were family.

God is close to us when we mourn. I believe in the vision of Revelation where God sits among us, wiping every tear from our eye. I believe in a place where the sting of death is gone, and there is only joy. We are a long way from the new heaven and earth where we will not grieve or feel any pain, though. We live in this broken and imperfect world. That does not mean, though, that we are alone.

On that summer afternoon, God was also next to a man stuffed into an uncomfortable waiting room chair. I believe that as he cried, God was there, not only wiping away the tears, but grieving the injustice with him. God dares to go to the places where human suffering is greatest, and to grieve with us.

Prayer

God, when the world does the worst it can, make your presence known. Sit next to us and grieve with us. Amen.

Chapter 54

BRAVE

"Be strong, and let us be courageous for the sake of our people, and for the cities of our God."

—2 Samuel 10:12a

Recently a newly out trans celebrity's photo appeared on a magazine cover. Immediately people online began to juxtapose her photo next to photos of veterans and first responders, saying that "real bravery" looked like the latter, and that trans people were not brave.

That is a false dichotomy. Bravery is not something that only those who have been in certain experiences can claim. Rather, bravery is the way in which we respond to situations that occur in our lives. Some make the front pages. Most do not.

Bravery is my father putting his family on a plane in Saigon in 1965, while he stayed behind. And bravery is my mother, twenty-six years old with two small children, waiting in the aftermath of an explosion in Vietnam for a call that took days to come telling her that her husband was alive.

Bravery is the person who finally stands up to a bully. And bravery is the bully who faces the person they have become and chooses to change.

Bravery is the politician who votes for an unpopular bill, even though they know it will cost them the election. And bravery is the citizen who lobbies for a bill they know will never be passed.

Bravery is a bunch of gays and trans folks seeking shelter together in a bar named Stonewall in 1969. And bravery is the young man who tells his evangelical parents, "I'm gay."

Bravery is allies standing up to bigots. And bravery is walking past armed men with guns so that you can pray in your own mosque.

Bravery is coming home from war. And bravery is the veteran who fights every day to stay alive.

Bravery is the firefighter who walks into their first burning building. And bravery is the family who picks up the pieces when their house burns down.

Bravery is the trans man who injects testosterone into his thigh for the first time. And bravery is the trans woman who says, "Call me by my name."

Bravery is not a contest. Bravery is a choice. True bravery is often hard to find. When we see it, no matter where, it should always be applauded.

Prayer

God, help me to be brave today, and help me to acknowledge the bravery of others. Amen.

Chapter 55

CRASHING THE BARRIERS

Then the high priest took action; he and all who were with him (that is, the sect of the Sadducees), being filled with jealousy, arrested the apostles and put them in the public prison. But during the night an angel of the Lord opened the prison doors, brought them out, and said, "Go, stand in the temple and tell the people the whole message about this life." When they heard this, they entered the temple at daybreak and went on with their teaching.

—Acts 5:17–21

Early one morning in June of 1969, police came to arrest the patrons of the Stonewall Bar in New York City. And in that moment, they did what few other LGBT people had ever done before: they refused to go quietly. That day was not the start of the LGBT rights movement, but it was a major early catalyst, which is why in most places we celebrate Pride weekends in June every year.

So what does this have to do with the book of Acts? At first glance, maybe not that much, but for me the stories of the early disciples remind me that there has always been a cost for those who wish to tell the truth about who they are, and what they believe. The disciples were jailed for testifying about their faith. But that's not the end of the story because Scripture tells us that the Lord refused to allow the fear of some to imprison God's people. And when morning came, the ones who would have kept the apostles captive got quite a shock. Not only could their fear not contain them, but more importantly they could not silence them.

Every time I come up against a barrier around sexuality or gender identity, I remember Stonewall. And I remember that even when we find ourselves held captive, either by the fears of others or ourselves, God can help us make a way back out into the light. Whether it's in a jail in Jerusalem, or a bar in New York City, or the very place our feet are planted in any moment, God is ready to set us free.

Prayer

God, thank you for calling us out from our fear and into the public places. Grant us the strength to not allow anything to hold us back from claiming the life you have in mind for us, and the love you give so graciously to us. Amen.

Chapter 56

AS A SON

*They were walking along, talking, when suddenly a
fiery chariot and fiery horses appeared and separated
the two of them. Then Elijah went to heaven in a
windstorm. Elisha was watching, and he cried out,
"Oh, my father, my father! Israel's chariots and its
riders!" When he could no longer see him, Elisha
took hold of his clothes and ripped them in two.*

—2 Kings 2:11–12 CEB

I believe in the idea of chosen family. That's no slight
to my family of origin, whom I love dearly. But I love
the idea that my family is made even larger by the fact
that there are people dear to my heart with whom I
share no legally binding connection.

LGBTQ people have long known about this concept. In fact, in decades past we have referred to other
LGBTQ folks as being "family." One of the reasons
why is that in a time when many families of origin
rejected their gay and trans kids, strong surrogate
families emerged instead. Thanksgivings and Christ-
mases were spent not back home, but in the protective
embrace of friends.

But chosen family doesn't belong to any one community. Elisha and Elijah knew that. Elijah was the
older mentor who taught Elisha, and who named him

his successor as prophet of Israel. Though not father and son by any legal measure, their relationship was in every way just as real. Elijah became Elisha's spiritual father, teaching him the faith and preparing him for his work.

It's no surprise, then, that when Elijah disappeared into a whirlwind, Elisha mourned as only a son would. In accordance with tradition, he took the clothes he was wearing, and ripped them in two.

Too often we limit our definitions of family. We include only those who share a last name or, worse, blood. But in the Bible, we see God working to create families in much broader ways. Jesus' important descent from King David comes not through a bloodline but through Joseph, his adoptive father. Ruth and Naomi cross religious lines to form family. John is told to see Mary as his own mother as Jesus hangs on the cross.

Our families teach us who we are, and who we can be. And sometimes God creates families for us in the most amazing ways.

Prayer

God, thank you for the family I have, no matter what binds us together. Amen.

Chapter 57

ALLOWING JOY

Rejoice in the Lord always; again I will say, Rejoice.
Let your gentleness be known to everyone. The Lord is
near. Do not worry about anything, but in everything
by prayer and supplication with thanksgiving let your
requests be made known to God. And the peace of
God, which surpasses all understanding, will guard
your hearts and your minds in Christ Jesus.

—Philippians 4:4–7

As a queer young activist in my late-teens and early-twenties, I believed that it was irresponsible to be joyful while injustice against LGBTQ flourished in the world. Happiness felt almost sinful while others suffered.

Later, when I became a person in recovery, I learned that it wasn't my responsibility to fix everything. And I also learned a lot about joy. I learned that though this world will always be imperfect, and while attention must be paid to that fact, there are often moments of extraordinary beauty and grace that require nothing less than our abundant joy.

Alice Walker wrote in *The Color Purple* that "I think it pisses God off if you walk by the color purple in a field somewhere and don't notice it."[2] My guess is it also pisses God off when we don't notice the goodness in our lives and give God our joy.

Paul wrote to the church in Philippi and told them to "rejoice." It's worth noting that he was likely writing his letter from a jail cell. If anyone had reason not to be joyful, it was Paul. And yet, even in the midst of injustice, he found reasons for joy and evidence of God's peace.

If that isn't resistance to the forces of evil in this world, I don't know what is.

Sometimes we who work for justice are so serious about doing what is right that we forget to also do what is good. I wonder what it would be like if we prioritized joy from time to time. My guess is that not only would the work still get done, but we would do it with more energy than ever before.

So, figure out what in your life is begging you to take notice, like purple in a field. And then, celebrate it. Thank God. Share it with others. Resist the idea that you cannot be joyful. And then, go and joyfully change the world.

Prayer

God, help me to be a joyful resister of whatever would distract me from the signs of your goodness. Amen.

Chapter 58

THROWN IN

Whoever digs a pit will fall into it; and whoever breaks through a wall will be bitten by a snake.

—Ecclesiastes 10:8

Recently I found myself with my wife's family on a large lake in central New York. Before we had left the dock, her teenaged cousin had convinced me to try her favorite activity, rafting at high speeds behind the boat. It had sounded fun back on dry land, but after seeing her take her first ride I was hesitant.

I stood looking behind the boat, assessing the strength of the raft that was now pulled up to the boat, wondering whether it could hold me, planning how I would get onto it, and looking for the ladder that would let me climb back up. I'm not a small person, and I was not sure how any of this would work. After counting all the ways I could potentially die, I decided that I would stay dry and perhaps try next time.

That's when the boat hit some choppy waves. My body launched to the right and towards the motor. To compensate, I threw myself to my left . . . landing safely on my back in the middle of the raft, bobbing and looking up at the blue sky.

"Well," I said, "I'm here—might as well give it a try."

I would be lying to you if I said this is something I'll be doing again anytime soon, but in the end, my brief high-speed journey behind the boat was a lot of fun. In a way, so was getting thrown off. We laughed the rest of the day at my attempts to navigate the tiny ladder out of the water. I was glad I did it. Once, anyway.

Like the writer of Ecclesiastes, I look for risk everywhere, certain that dangers lurk behind every corner. Caution and good sense are always appropriate. Sometimes, though, I need a little push that gets me out of my head and to the new things that deep down I really want to try. When that happens, I find I'm rarely disappointed.

Do I think God sent the wave that rocked the boat that put me on that raft? No. But do I think that God saw the joy and laughter of a cautious middle-ager and laughed along with me? In my heart, I have no doubt.

Prayer

God, when I get thrown into a new opportunity, throw yourself there with me. Calm my fear and share my joy. Amen.

Chapter 59

ALLIGATORS AND ICE

*An intelligent mind acquires knowledge, and
the ear of the wise seeks knowledge.*

—Proverbs 18:15

Moving to Florida as a child had been enough of a shock for me before the reptile presentation. Sitting in my third-grade classroom, the guest speaker circulated pamphlets with full-color photos of Florida's abundance of venomous snakes. That was nothing, though, compared to the alligator talk.

Should one ever be chased by an alligator, they explained in a tone that suggested this was a rather common occurrence, there was a simple remedy: just run in a zigzag formation, and they will be unable to follow you. Years later I learned that this advice was disproved. I'm scared to ask how. Perhaps the gators caught on.

There are no gators where I live now. What we do have, though, is an overabundance of cold weather. It covers our cars with snow, coats the sidewalks with ice, and unleashes biting wind that feels like it blows right through you.

My first few years in New England, I did not navigate this well. I bought the wrong jackets, slipped down sidewalks, and rear-ended another car in the snow. The gators started to look good. It wasn't until I met my now-wife, born and raised with the lake-effect snow of western New York, that I started to learn what she had known her whole life: buy the warmer coat, walk like a penguin on ice, leave more room between cars when it's snowing.

I sometimes hear from members of the LGBTQ community my age and up that so much has changed since we came out. When teenagers call themselves "queer," folks who had that term hurled at them as an insult recoil. When college students come home using they/them pronouns, some scratch their heads in bafflement, wondering why "he" and "she" aren't good enough anymore. It's almost like we learned all the dangers of a gator-filled world only to be met with a nor'easter we never saw coming.

Proverbs reminds us that our quest for knowledge and understanding never ends. More than just a desire to be intelligent, it's a divine calling. When our world changes around us, we can choose to stay out in the cold, freezing to death while looking for gators that will never come. Or, we have the option of learning something new, and finding the beauty and wonder of a whole new landscape.

Prayer

God, when you change the world around us for good, help us to change how we respond to it too. (And help us to outrun those gators.) Amen.

Chapter 60

MASTERPIECES

"For I know the plans I have for you," declares the LORD,
"plans to prosper you and not to harm you, plans to
give you hope and a future. Then you will call on me
and come and pray to me, and I will listen to you."

—Jeremiah 29:11–12 NIV

The first Christmas after we were married, my wife
Heidi and I put up the tree, wrapped the lights around
it, and then broke open a box filled with Christmas
ornaments from her childhood. One caught my attention. It had a picture of her as an infant and said,
"Baby's First Christmas, 1983." After I looked at it
for a minute, I realized something wasn't right.

"Honey, 1983 wasn't your first Christmas. You
were born in October of 1982. Why does it say 1983?"

And then I remembered. Heidi was born three
months premature. She weighed slightly over two
pounds at birth and slipped down to under two
pounds soon after that. Baptized at the hospital soon
after birth, she wasn't expected to survive, and spent
her first few months in a hospital incubator. She was
released from the hospital right before Christmas but
was still so fragile that celebrations had to take a back
seat that year.

By the next year she was strong and healthy and growing. Christmas was a little different that year. Someone took the picture of her that is now on our tree, and put it in a frame that said "Baby's First Christmas." Is it technically right? No. But the reality was that it was the first Christmas that her family could breathe a sigh of relief, know that she was going to be OK, and rejoice. It was the first year that they had time to buy ornaments and take festive pictures to put inside of them.

When I look at the ornament, I think of Heidi on her actual first Christmas: tiny, fragile, sick, and struggling to live. But I also think about the strength that must have been inside that little body, and the hope that she gave people against all the odds. I know that God was with Heidi in that NICU bassinet, just as I know God has been framing her beautiful life every day since.

For those of us who are queer or trans, our milestones sometimes don't fit the ready-made frames of the world. We are often on our own timelines, coming more into ourselves in our own time. Too often, like the doctors who said Heidi wouldn't survive, the world seems to say to us, "You'll never make it."

To live as queer or trans is to be aware of our vulnerability, and of the fragility of the world. So, when we find ourselves thriving, we have a particular reason to celebrate. The frames we choose to share our pride may need a little more explanation than others, but the backstory is all the better for it.

Prayer

God, you have created a masterpiece in me. Help me to choose the frame that tells my story with joy and without shame. Amen.

Chapter 61

HOLY GROUNDS

"Do not come any closer," God said.
"Take off your sandals, for the place where
you are standing is holy ground."

—Exodus 3:5 NIV

There is a Christian tradition about the spot where Jesus was born. A church in Bethlehem sits over the very spot where Jesus was said to have laid in a manger. It is considered so holy that three different Christian traditions, one Catholic and two Orthodox, have laid claim to it for centuries. Monks from each tradition live there in a sort of an uneasy truce. The monks still sometimes even have fist fights over the space.

I don't think that's what Jesus wants for the place he was born. I'm not even sure if that is the exact place he was born or not, or if it even matters. But what I am sure of is that we want to remember that place where Christ was first born. We remember it enough to want to know exactly where it was, and to keep that place as holy ground.

But as holy as we consider Bethlehem, I wonder if our understanding of holy ground has to be limited to the places we find in the Bible? Or do we all have holy ground places in our lives?

A few years ago, I was flying into Atlanta, where I spent my late teens and twenties. As we descended, I was listening to an Indigo Girls album that had come out when I was in college there. The music and memories welled up inside me, with the lights from the city shining below. The beautiful feelings of freedom I had first felt there resurfaced, and I remembered what a gift coming out in that time and place had been.

I love church buildings and think that they are incredibly valuable and necessary spaces for communities of faith. But I know that each of us has places where we feel the closest to God's love. For LGBTQ people who have long felt unsafe in church buildings, it is especially important to affirm those spaces. Maybe they are cities. Maybe they are beaches. Maybe they are mountains. Wherever they are, they are holy, because God is already there.

If we who are waiting for Christ treated every space as hallowed ground, how would the world look different? What fights would we stop having? What peace could we share with others? And how often could we remind ourselves that no matter where we go, we are still in God's presence?

The world is full of holy spaces. Rest assured, God is already there waiting for you around every corner.

Prayer

God, you are already in the places I am going. Let me meet you there with awe and know that I am on holy ground. Amen.

Chapter 62

ANOTHER WAY

And having been warned in a dream not to return to Herod, they left for their own country by another road.

—Matthew 2:12

My initial meeting with the pastoral search committee of the first church I served was in the middle of a Vermont winter. I drove across the border of a state I'd never been to before and followed my GPS as it led me past ice fishing shacks, up mountains, and into a snow-covered valley. After the interview I turned the GPS back on, and it took me a slightly different way. I drove through unpaved roads right outside the Green Mountain National Forest, following turn by turn, until I came to a sign posted on the road:

"Your GPS is wrong! Road closed in winter months."

I turned around, with the automated voice of my GPS guy yelling angrily at me to turn back the other way. Eventually I made my way back home, but that sign stuck with me for some time. Without it, I would have gone down the road and, with my Southerner's driving skills, probably would have gotten stuck in the snow.

When I moved to the town, I learned how that road became impassible each winter, and that the sign had been put up to keep others from getting into dangerous situations. It struck me as a good-hearted act of kindness that the locals had put up that sign for strangers.

When the magi left the manger, they knew the easy road to take. They also knew it led back to Herod, and to danger for the newborn Christ. So, they found a new way home, one wide enough for the new understanding they had of God, and for both the joy and challenge it would bring.

I also like that Vermont sign because it reminds me that the journey doesn't always turn out the way we think it will. We might put our trust in the "sure things," like a good GPS, but in the end, life throws up its share of curves in the road. Sometimes the wisest thing we can do is to ignore the directions we have been given and apply what we learn from others on our journey.

Many of us who are queer or trans grew up in an era of set roadmaps, literally and figuratively. We had turn-by-turn directions for how to navigate gender and sexuality: basically, stay on the main roads and don't go exploring. Having spent my life off-roading gender, I'll admit that the paved road sometimes looks a lot easier. I've certainly heard the angry GPS voice of conformity telling me to turn back around. I've come to understand, though, that no one knows the terrain better than the locals, and when it comes to knowing who I am, I'm the best navigator of the land.

Prayer

God, even when you send me on the backroads, help me to trust that you will show me the way and make my paths wide enough for me to see the fullness of your love. Amen.

Chapter 63

EVERYDAY SAINTS

Here is a call for the endurance of the saints,
those who keep the commandments of God
and hold fast to the faith of Jesus.

—Revelation 14:12

I believe that saints continue to live among us, recognized or not. There are people of exceptional goodness and mercy and justice whose legacy we often do not understand until they are gone.

No one is asking me to nominate people to sainthood, but if they did, I think my first choice would be a man named Mychal Judge. Father Judge was a Roman Catholic priest, a Franciscan, and a chaplain for the New York City Fire Department. In death he became known to many as one of the first fatalities on 9/11. Father Judge had responded to the scene as part of his fire chaplain duties. He was struck by falling debris while praying and died on the scene.

What is truly memorable about Father Judge is not the way he died. It's how he lived. Throughout his life, Father Judge was a friend to politicians and to the powerful. And he was also a friend to the poor and the down-and-out. He began ministering to people with AIDS in the earliest days of the epidemic, and he maintained an active ministry to those in recovery from addictions. He seemed to be a priest for all people; one who was able to see God in everyone he met.

In the aftermath of his death, more of his story was shared. Father Judge was in recovery from addiction himself, and open to his friends about the fact he was gay and (though, like monks of all sexual orientations, faithful to his vow of celibacy) comfortable with himself. I would have liked to have met him, and to have heard about what was certainly a "dark night of the soul" that brought him from addiction to a life of deep joy.

There's one story from his life that stays with me in particular. A fellow Franciscan says Father Judge used to ask him, "You know what I need?" And the other priest would say, "No" and listen for a suggestion of what he could get for his friend. He'd ask again, "You know what I really need?" And then Father Judge would say, "Absolutely nothing. I don't need a thing in the world. I am the happiest man on the face of the earth."

Most of us are not called to a life of chastity, poverty, and obedience, but all of us are called to a life of joy. Joy does not stand in opposition to God's plan for our lives; I truly believe it is an essential part of God's plan. When we find someone who has lived with that joy so vividly, and with such a clear heart for the people of God, then we know for sure that we have found a saint.

Prayer

God, we are all just saints in training, but some of us are master students. Help us to recognize them by their joy, and to learn from them when we can. Amen.

Chapter 64

OPEN TO REARRANGING

A new heart I will give you, and a new spirit I will put within you; and I will remove from your body the heart of stone and give you a heart of flesh.

—Ezekiel 36:26

Until I was 35, I spent my adulthood living alone. I liked having my own space. Everything had its rightful place, and I knew just how to find it. Then, I fell in love. A few months before the wedding, my wife-to-be moved in.

One day I came home from a long meeting. I'd been away all day, and I was trying to catch up on things around the house, so I started to put some clean dishes away. Except, nothing was right. The silverware was in a new drawer. The plates had changed cabinets. The pots and pans were AWOL. And so, I stood in the kitchen, casserole dish in hand, and did the only logical thing: I got mad at my fiancée and said, "Why is nothing in the right place?"

It was, of course, not logical to get mad at her. I generally use the kitchen only to make coffee, while she is a great cook who whips up delicious dinners for us both. She had rearranged the kitchen in a way that made sense to a cook and not to a bachelor who preferred the counter at the local diner. And, beyond that, there were far better ways to voice my confusion than to grumble at her. It was not my finest moment.

After I apologized, I thought about my reaction. Change, even in small increments, can be a huge stressor. Our equilibrium gets knocked out from under us, and we have to adjust. Even when it's change for the good, sometimes we lash out at the change-makers. At best our relationships suffer, and at worst we become resistant to letting anyone in who might disturb our carefully curated balance.

In the end, though, we might just find that the change is worth it. That day I got frustrated, I failed to see that my fiancée had spent the afternoon cooking my favorite soup and making dessert. I was so caught up in the fact that things weren't the way they had always been that I missed all the good stuff. I'm aware that I probably do that far too often in my life. I think a lot of us do.

These days, I keep looking for the new life that God continues to offer to us when the old way isn't working anymore. The more I learn to let go, the more I find the joy in what comes next—at home, at church, in community, and everywhere. I still don't always know where the casserole dish goes, but I always know that there will be someone there, ready to show me.

Prayer

God, never let my fear of change stop me from accepting the joy you bring us through others. Amen.

Chapter 65

"GOOD TROUBLE"

The Lord is good, a stronghold in a day of trouble.

—Nahum 1:7a

In 1996, the Atlanta Pride parade was making its way down Peachtree Street in the suffocating heat. Our contingent was small, even though my college was one of the largest institutions in the city. Being out was a risk everywhere back then, especially in the South. Undeterred, a handful of us carried a banner and marched through Midtown, turning finally to make our entry into Piedmont Park.

As we approached, a man stood waving to the marchers, cheering them on. It was John Lewis, our local congressman and veteran of the civil rights movement. This was the man who had crossed the Edmund Pettus Bridge in Selma, Alabama, with Dr. King, despite being beaten. This was the man who spoke at the March on Washington in 1963. He was a true moral hero, and here he was, cheering us on.

My respect for Congressman Lewis has only grown with time. The phrase "good trouble" would become synonymous with his name in later years. He would give generations of new justice-seekers an understanding of their work in a world that would push back, and call them no good, just as the world had done to him thirty years before.

There was a great concert that year at Pride. We sang our hearts out to the Indigo Girls and stayed out late. We went home exhausted and joyful. But nothing that day brought greater joy than seeing the congressman there, clapping as we rounded the corner. It became clear that our struggle for equality was bound up in all the other struggles for equality through the ages, and that none of us had to fight our battles alone.

John Lewis was a man of deep Christian faith. His beliefs drove what he did. I believe they even brought him to that corner that day, allowing him to do a little preaching to us all while hardly saying a word.

There are times when members of other groups face injustice, and I am tempted to sit back and say, "I did my time in the trenches—let the new generation handle this one." Then I remember that a man far greater than I stood in the June heat and celebrated us at a time when few would. None of us gets to sit back while the struggle continues. All of us are called to the parade.

Prayer

God, help me to get into "good trouble," not just for myself, but especially for others. Amen.

Chapter 66

MANDATE

"I give you a new commandment, that you love one another. Just as I have loved you, you also should love one another. By this everyone will know that you are my disciples, if you have love for one another."

—John 13:34–35

The night before he died, Jesus knew what was going to happen. By the end of the night, one of his disciples would betray him to the authorities, one would deny him three times, and all of them would leave him alone in his hour of greatest pain. Even still, he gathered them all around the table, broke bread and shared wine, and told his disciples to keep doing it, even after he was gone.

What do you do if you're Jesus? What do you do if you know you are not going to be around much longer, and you have to tell the people you love the most—the ones who followed you, the ones who sometimes make big mistakes—how to keep moving in the right direction after you're gone?

Every year on Maundy Thursday, three days before Easter, we remember his answer and that first Lord's Supper. We also read the Scripture for today, filled with the words from that last evening together. Each year on this night, clergy are also asked one question more than any other: What does "Maundy" mean?

It comes from a Latin word: *mandatum*. Mandatum means "mandate" or a "commandment." And when we talk about "Maundy Thursday," we're talking about "mandate Thursday." We're talking about the night that Christ told his disciples exactly what he expected of them.

The final thing Christ really wanted his disciples to know was how others would know who they followed: Not by a Christian fish sticker on a car, or a cross around the neck; not by the anger some Christians express on the evening news, or the mean-spiritedness others show in their day-to-day lives; but simply by his mandate: to love.

In the end, the world did its worst to Jesus. The resurrection surely came on Sunday, but in a real way it started on Thursday night, with love's refusal to die. Christ's words are a story about what happens when love meets violence and hatred and fear, and yet love wins anyway. It's a story of love that was rejected and buried, and yet was still too strong to stay in the ground.

For those of us who have been condemned for our love, Christ reminds us of his real law. Though the world too often does its worst, there is hope for us yet.

Prayer

God, you gave your church one job. May we do our work with the love you require. Amen.

Chapter 67

HOLY SCHISMS

"[T]hat they may all be one."

—John 17:21a

A few years ago, I watched as a large mainline denomination moved closer to a possible split around LGBTQ inclusion. Meetings began happening to propose a way forward that included the option of amicable separation. In their wake, many folks (mostly straight and cisgender, incidentally), decried the news, saying that the church should never schism.

The reality is that the church of Jesus Christ has been in schism for over a thousand years, and many of those schisms have been necessary and good. The Protestant Reformation was a schism. American denominations were in schism during the Civil War, with the Presbyterians not reuniting until 1983 and Baptists remaining divided. Other denominations have broken apart over the inclusion of women. The truth is that schism is practically as old as the church.

And it's not necessarily a bad thing.

Here's how I think of churches that break apart over issues of inclusion: everyone is in a large room, and there is one big table. The trouble is, not everyone seated at the table agrees that everyone else should be allowed to sit. So, the ones who aren't allowed to sit remain standing against the wall while everyone else sits comfortably, eats well, and debates whether they will let the ones standing sit at the table.

True allies quickly reach a point where they say, "We aren't going to wait for our friends to be allowed to sit anymore." They stand up, giving up the seat their privilege affords them, and stand with their friends.

This isn't the moment of schism. This is the realization that the church is already in schism because a church is not whole that does not recognize the baptisms of all of its members. This is the recognition that some of the folks who had been left standing against the wall have given up and left the room entirely. There is no sin in good allies pointing out the shame in that and demanding that it is time to adjust the seating arrangements accordingly.

I still do pray for a time when "they may all be one." Because we are humans, and deeply fallible, I fear that may not come about on earth. It may only be in the next life, when we see God's love and truth face-to-face. When we reach that place, I pray that the seating arrangements are better for everyone, and the table big enough for us all.

Prayer

God, may I never worship consensus more than I worship you, and may I never settle for a compromise that leaves others without a seat at the table. Amen.

Chapter 68

GETTING IT WRONG

"There is no one who is righteous, not even one."

—Romans 3:10

I read *To Kill a Mockingbird* the summer between eighth and ninth grade. It was a hot, Southern summer and I went into a bookstore to look for some indoor reading. I took it home and devoured it.

I was transformed, both in a moral and literary sense. I would never forget the idea that standing up for the right thing, even when you know you are going to lose, is noble. Even today, Harper Lee's book is on my shortlist of favorite novels.

We even have a cat named "Atticus."

Years later, *Go Set a Watchman,* a sort of early draft of the book, was released and I was ecstatic. But when I read about the book, my heart ached a bit. This version of Atticus attended a Klan rally. He spoke against integration, and he did not consider Black people equal. He asked Scout, "Do you want them in our world?"[3] Atticus Finch, it turned out, wasn't such a good guy after all.

Distraught, I called out, "Honey, can we change the cat's name?" (The answer was "no.")

With time, though, I wonder if a legion of Atticus Finch fans having to come to terms with his racism isn't the best possible thing for us all.

Though I try my best to be an ally in the fight against racism, the reality is that all of us, even the best-intentioned white allies, need to wrestle with the racism inside our ourselves. Even before the new book, my willingness to so easily buy into the white-savior narrative of Atticus was an indication of that. We all internalize the injustice of the world, and we all wrestle with unlearning our prejudices.

Atticus Finch was not a Dr. King, or Bayard Rustin, or Rosa Parks, or Medgar Evers. That's OK, because that's not the role of an ally anyway. An ally is not a hero. An ally is a supporter. That's true not only of the racial justice struggle, but the LGBTQ movement as well.

Instead, Atticus was the character who inspired many of us in our younger years to try to do what was right. He made us take a hard look at ourselves and ask whether we could be courageous. Perhaps his greatest legacy as a character, with all that has now been revealed and with all that our country now faces, would be for all of us to search our hearts once again.

Prayer

God your love is perfect. My love is not. Give me the courage to be an ally, and the humility to know when I mess up. Amen.

Chapter 69

UNEVEN GIFTS

*[Jesus] said also to the one who had invited him,
"When you give a luncheon or a dinner, do
not invite your friends or your brothers or your
relatives or rich neighbors, in case they may invite
you in return, and you would be repaid."*

—Luke 14:12

Every couple of weeks I have lunch with a good friend of mine. Early in our friendship we struck up a pattern of alternating who paid. So, about once a month I'd pay, and once a month she would take the check.

Earlier this year we were both busy and missed a few months of lunches. We were finally able to reschedule, but as I pulled up to the restaurant, I realized I had no idea whose "turn" it was to pay for lunch. I tried to remember where we had gone and who had pulled out their wallet first, but I just could not seem to place it.

My fear was not that I would accidentally pay for a lunch I did not owe. My fear was that I would not pay my fair share.

I think a lot of us have that fear. We believe in sending thank you notes and keeping careful track of who gave us a birthday gift so that we can reciprocate. And while most of that is about having good manners, at least a small part might be this: we don't want to owe anybody anything.

Maybe that's why grace is so hard for us sometimes. We as Christians know, at least intellectually, that we are people who have received grace. We did not earn grace. We did not work our way to it. We got it for free. And as wonderful as that is, it's also deeply distressing. Because, ultimately, that means it is not ours, and we cannot control it. And yet, we can respond to it.

I live a life that is in so many ways easier and more joyful because of what previous generations of out LGBTQ folks did for my generation. I can get married, visit my wife in the hospital, dress in a way that reflects my gender, and insist that others use my correct pronouns. I have received grace upon grace. There is no way I can ever repay those earlier generations, many of whom suffered greatly for their witness.

Our Reformed forebearers have for centuries taught that the only proper response to grace is gratitude. We don't do good and generous things in order that we might earn grace. We don't do these things with an expectation of a greater gift, or of repayment. We do good and generous things because we are thankful, and because we can never pay a gift this big back.

And so, we pay it forward.

Prayer

God of grace, thank you for all that we have been given. And thank you that we will never be able to repay it. Help us instead to find new ways to say "thank you" to this incredible gift. Amen.

Chapter 70

FORGIVING THE CHILD

God heals the brokenhearted and binds up their wounds.

—Psalm 147:3

A few years back, someone I respected and cared about did something hurtful to me. In the aftermath I searched for reconciliation and resolution to no avail. It was a bewildering and painful time; one I'm still in somewhat.

What helped me was remembering a teaching I'd once read from Buddhist leader Thich Nhat Hanh. I'm far from a Buddhist practitioner or scholar, but this one resonated with me. He was talking about forgiving those who hurt us and using the metaphorical example of a father and a wounded son.

He asked the "sons," who could be any of us, to try to imagine who the father had been as a five-year-old, and to give them compassion. That's hard enough, but then came the tougher part. He encouraged them to see that five-year-old, and imagine the ways they have been hurt, and how it has shaped them. He then asked them to have compassion for that five-year-old who would grow to hurt them.

Jesus Christ told us to "let the little children come to me" (Mark 10:14). When someone hurts me, particularly someone who has been hurt by the injustices of the world, I try to think of them as a child. I think of the ways that they were hurt, of the fears they still carry because of it, and of the pain they still might live in daily. When I'm able to do that, I'm able to find compassion, even when I am hurting myself. I picture myself kneeling down, asking that five-year-old if they want a hug, and showing them the compassion they never received.

Many, if not all of us, carry scared, hurt children inside. As adults it is our job to do the work of healing that is necessary so that we do not then pass those hurts on to others. Sometimes, though, it is also our job to find ways to welcome the wounded child in others, and to find it in us to give that wounded part of them our compassion.

It's lifelong work, and every time I'm asked to do it, it's painful. I remember the words of the Psalm, though, and the God who knows every part of my history, and every part of theirs as well. Both I and those who hurt me, both I and those whom I have hurt, are equally known and beloved by God. There will come a day when we meet again in God's kingdom, and we will know perfect reconciliation. For now, I just try to get ready for that time, and to practice messy and imperfect compassion here on earth.

Prayer

Dear God, I see the pain of those who hurt me. I see who they were when they were hurt. I refuse to withhold my compassion any longer. Amen.

Chapter 71

TENDING THE TREE

"No good tree bears bad fruit, nor again does a bad tree bear good fruit; for each tree is known by its own fruit."

—Luke 6:43–45

Often, we are asked to turn inward, and to reflect spiritually on ourselves. That's certainly not a bad thing. Any thoughtful and faithful person should do that. When it comes to deep introspection, though, the isolated individual is not always the whole story. We do not take our spiritual journeys alone, so why don't we spend more time as Christians looking at our whole communities as well?

Jesus reminds us we cannot expect good fruit from a tree that has gone bad. If our roots are failing, if our soil goes unwatered, or if the branches are withering, no shiny apples or robust pears are soon to come. But if the tree itself is healthy, if it is pruned with care and treated with love, it cannot help but bear good and nourishing fruit.

Alcoholics Anonymous groups sometimes have what is called a "group conscience" meeting. They reflect honestly on the health of their group, acknowledge wrongs, and look for spiritual direction on how to do better. It's a process I wish more communities, including churches, would consider.

This is especially true for those of us who have been hurt by the church. As much as we would never want to pass that pain on to others, sometimes it is only too easy to recreate those same familiar patterns in new places. Some of the most abusive and authoritarian churches I've seen, unfortunately, have also been some of the most progressive, filled with people who believe they have escaped their past.

It's always a good time to reflect on the communities that we are a part of, and ask whether they are healthy, or whether they need a little extra care. Are our congregations kind and compassionate places? Are our denominations centering their identity in Christ and seeking God's righteousness? Are our communities of all sorts the kinds of places that can grow good fruit?

Too often our rugged individualism convinces us that we just need to improve ourselves. Christians know, however, that God does not call us out alone. Christ calls us into community with one another. Examining our beloved communities is rarely easy work, but it is necessary. We are but the branches of a tree much larger than ourselves. The environment in which we are growing matters. If we hope to bear good fruit, we start with taking care of the tree itself.

Prayer

God, help me to care not just for the fruit, and not just for the branch, but for the whole tree. Amen.

Chapter 72

WHEN TO START TALKING

It is not enemies who taunt me— I could bear that;
it is not adversaries who deal insolently with
me—I could hide from them.
But it is you, my equal, my companion,
my familiar friend,
with whom I kept pleasant company.

—Psalm 55:12–14

Dr. Martin Luther King once said, "In the end, we will remember not the words of our enemies, but the silence of our friends."[4] In other words, when we are in times of crisis, it won't be our attackers with their taunts who will haunt us. Instead, it will be those we believed to be allies, the ones we thought would come to our aid, whose inaction we will remember.

Have you ever had a friend let you down like that? In a time when others are speaking badly about you, that friend couldn't be found. Or, they were there but didn't say a word in your defense? What hurt more? The things being said about you, or your friend's betrayal?

I think we've all had a friend like that at least once in our lives. More importantly, though, I think we've all been that friend. When we've had a chance to speak up for our friends, or for people like them, we've kept our mouths shut and hoped the moment would pass quickly. And in that moment, whether we've realized it or not, we've hurt our friends more than any words could have.

We live in an age where we are sometimes defined less by our words than by our silences. If we say "Black Lives Matter" to our Black friends, yet keep our mouths shut when our racist uncle utters a slur at Thanksgiving dinner, we aren't really being allies. If we say that we support the "Me Too" movement on social media yet dismiss accounts of harassment or support in our social circles, we aren't being true friends to the ones who need friends the most. If we say "Love is Love" among our friends yet vote for those who would deny equal rights to all, we aren't being honest with our own love.

But a true friend? A true friend stands up and fills the silence with a call to justice. A true friend risks something because the friendship matters to them. A true friend will be remembered, for days to come, for what they did when it was needed the most.

Prayer

God, make me the person who speaks up for my friends, both when they're around, and when they're not. Amen.

Chapter 73

RENEWED FOR RESISTANCE

For everything there is a season, and a time for every matter under heaven.

—Ecclesiastes 3:1

On the Monday of the week when this country reached the point of actual children being held in actual cages at the US/Mexico border (or at least the week the general public became aware of it), I found myself fly fishing on a river near another border: the Canadian one.

As I drove north from my home, I passed a Border Patrol checkpoint on the interstate. Each southbound car was being pulled over and each passenger asked about their citizenship status. I drove on, knowing my driver's license and passport card were safely tucked into my wallet, and that I could pass by easily.

Standing in the river later that day, I felt the weight of privilege press in on me. I didn't have to worry about borders. I have not (yet) been threatened with my own cage. I had the means and resources to take a few days away from my work to do nothing more than fish. I would return to a comfortable home and the loving embrace of my legally recognized (for now) family.

I felt guilty that in a time when there is so much pain, I should have so much comfort. And yet, as I looked out at the river, rolling by me in a never-ending current, and at the trees and sky, and even at the beautiful colors of the rainbow trout I released back into icy-cold waters, I felt something else too: joy. God's creation is too beautiful to not appreciate when we see it, and too awe-inspiring to not be taken seriously as well.

So much of surviving in this difficult time depends on our ability to sustain ourselves for the work yet to come. There is enough work to do to keep us occupied every minute of every day. And yet, if we burn out now, in the early innings, the powers of oppression and death will prevail well before the game is over.

By Wednesday morning I was back at the work of "resisting the powers of oppression and evil" as our baptismal vows read. I did my work with a renewed mind and body, and a spirit full of courage and faith. I'd like to think that I did better work for the fact I'd had a little rest and a little joy.

This will be a long journey of resistance. We are going to need everyone for every step of the way. Do the things that let you keep marching. Take the trip. Take the nap. Take pleasure in the joyful things you love. They will help you to keep going, and they will remind you that God is always with us, on the seas, on the rivers, and everywhere.

Prayer

God, in the midst of the toughest days, may I still find glimpses of joy. Amen.

Chapter 74

ASKING FOR WISDOM

*The fear of the LORD is the beginning of
wisdom; all those who practice it have a good
understanding. God's praise endures forever.*

—Psalm 111:10

A few years ago, I began adding something new to
my prayers every evening. Instead of asking for things
to work out the way I wanted, or for nothing to go
wrong, I began to pray instead for wisdom. That one
small change to my prayer life has made a tremendous difference in my life.

Back then I had been reading the story of Solomon
in Scripture, and I was struck that when God asked
Solomon what he wanted, he didn't asked for wealth,
or power, or success. Instead, he just wanted wisdom.
And, Scripture tells us, God was so impressed with
Solomon's request that God gave him all the things he
hadn't asked for as well.

In the Serenity Prayer we pray for the "serenity
to accept the things we cannot change, courage to
change the things we can, and the wisdom to know
the difference." It's that last line that is the kicker for
me, especially when the work of making the earth as
it is in heaven feels so heavy. Knowing what we can
change, and what we cannot, is crucial to our spiritual

life. Wisdom helps us to decide between acceptance and action. It either moves us to peace or prods us to change the world.

The Psalm tells us that wisdom is rooted in the "fear of the Lord." We are not talking about the kind of fear here that makes us cower from God's judgment. Instead, it's a kind of awe that opens our soul up to something greater than we could ever imagine. When we turn to face God and find ourselves unable to comprehend the magnitude of what we encounter, that's when we realize that we could never ask for any gift as profound as wisdom.

I do not think that I am wise. Not yet at least. But I do believe that my path has become clearer these past years. I know a little more about what I'm supposed to do in my day-to-day life. At the end of the day, that's possibly the greatest gift that prayer has ever given to me.

Prayer

God, if I may only have one thing, then please grant me wisdom. Amen.

Chapter 75

TESTIFY

*O give thanks to the L*ORD*, for God is good;*
for God's steadfast love endures forever.

*Let the redeemed of the L*ORD *say so, those God*
redeemed from trouble, and gathered in.

—Psalm 107:1–3a

We don't talk about testimony much in the more progressive branches of Christianity. One rarely "testifies" to the goodness of God in their lives within the confines of our churches. We who are the "frozen chosen" prefer to leave that to other churches.

I didn't learn about testimony from the church. I learned about it from other LGBTQ people in the addiction recovery community who told me their stories when I was newly sober. Again and again, they told me about what their lives had been like, and how God had intervened. Rising up from rock bottom, leaning on the grace of God, they built lives of meaning and purpose.

I needed those testimonies. I needed something to believe when it felt like God was so far away. Without them, I don't know what would have happened.

I sometimes wonder what testimonies the people in our pews need to hear. Do they need to hear someone say that there is life after the marriage implodes?

Do they search for an assurance that chemo was hard for everyone else too? Do they want to know what it was like for someone else when they stepped out in faith and used the pronouns that felt right to them for the first time?

I think ministers should preach often and well, but I sometimes wonder if we need to loosen our grip on the pulpit from time to time. Maybe there are some testimonies that we need to step aside and let be heard. Maybe the redeemed of the Lord need to be able to "say so."

There are as many stories of redemption as there are people surrounding you in the pews on Sunday. Church should be a place where our stories are not hidden but are shared for others to hear. God has given you a story to tell; do not be afraid to tell it.

Prayer

God, you have redeemed me. Help me to tell my story, that through me you might redeem another. Amen.

Chapter 76

ARMORED

Put on God's armor so that you can make a stand against the tricks of the devil. We aren't fighting against human enemies but against rulers, authorities, forces of cosmic darkness, and spiritual powers of evil in the heavens.

—Ephesians 6:11–12 CEB

Right after this passage comes the well-known "put on the armor of God" Scripture. We are encouraged to wear the "belt of truth," "breastplate of justice," and "shield of faith." I have always struggled with that passage. I don't like the image of militarized Christianity much, and I never want to encourage the idea of Crusade-like armies.

I do, however, like the idea of standing up to "rulers, authorities, forces of cosmic darkness, and spiritual powers of evil." We live in a world where too much power is given to those who should not have it. Walter Wink wrote about these "powers and principalities" and talked about how our true allegiance must never be to them, but to Christ.[5] The good news of our faith is that help is coming. God is daring to break into our world once again, and to stand with us. It doesn't matter how well-armed the world may be; the peace of Christ will always prevail in the end.

The only trouble for us is that until that happens, we must survive. For LGBTQ folks, our survival has never been something we can simply take for granted, physically and emotionally, but also spiritually. When it comes to our spiritual lives, queer and trans folks need what the armor of God can provide.

This is not the armor that one puts on to go into battle. This is the armor that keeps us safe while we keep doing the everyday work of following Christ. We walk through the work clothed in truth, justice, faith, and peace. We shrug off every arrow that comes our way. We choose a different path.

To be God's people, to refuse to be won over by the violence of powers and principalities, is more devastating to the established order than any war we could wage. To choose instead to walk with Christ in this world, while being our full selves, is an act of courage. When war is too often being waged against us by our fellow Christians, we choose a different way because we know that our witness has the power to strike a true death blow against the false powers of the world.

Prayer

God, help me to walk through the world unarmed but always protected by you. Amen.

Chapter 77

UNCOMFORTABLE

*We are putting no obstacle in anyone's way, so that
no fault may be found with our ministry, but as
servants of God we have commended ourselves in
every way: through great endurance, in afflictions,
hardships, calamities, beatings, imprisonments,
riots, labors, sleepless nights, [and] hunger.*

—2 Corinthians 6:3–5

On my first day of preaching class back in seminary,
the professor read this passage and then he said,
"That's what the first Christians endured in order to
preach the Gospel . . . you'll probably survive this
class."

Sometimes we contemporary Christians make
the mistake of thinking we have it rough. We have
to compete with Sunday morning baseball games
and yoga classes. Our pews aren't full the way they
were back in 1950. Our kids can't even sing "Silent
Night" at school anymore! Some even say that modern American Christians are being "persecuted."

Except, really, we modern American Christians
are pretty darn comfortable. And don't tell the angry
pundits on Fox News who are railing against "can-
cel culture" and trans kids playing sports, but calling
yourself Christian in our culture is one of the easiest

things you can do. It can even win you votes, business, and friends. Conversely, not being Christian can cost you dearly.

That's too bad, because the church does not do well when things are easy for it. Look back at nearly every time the church has been on the wrong side of history: the Crusades, the Spanish Inquisition, slavery, homophobia. What do all these have in common? When each happened, the church was in a position of great strength and influence in society.

But on the other hand, look at the times churches got it right: Black Christians in the Civil Rights movement. Dietrich Bonhoeffer and the Confessing Church in Nazi Germany. Oscar Romero standing at the altar. They, along with their churches, were hated, targeted, outnumbered, and sometimes they may as well have signed their own death warrants. But they were being the church in a way few of us ever will.

The church does not thrive in comfort. The church thrives when it is being called to the messy and painful work of transforming the world. The good news for the church is that it is blessed with LGBTQ Christians who have lived with discomfort and know how to thrive anyway. One of our gifts to the body of Christ is our witness to the One who transcends all the injustice of the world, and who gives us strength to teach a new way.

Prayer

O God, please make the church uncomfortable enough to once again do our best work. Amen.

Chapter 78

GRACE FOR THE LATECOMERS

"When those hired about five o'clock came, each of them received the usual daily wage. Now when the first came, they thought they would receive more; but each of them also received the usual daily wage."

—Matthew 20:9–10

In 2001 I was ordained as a minister in the Presbyterian Church. At that time the denomination was hotly debating the ordination of LGB folks (there was very little discussion of trans matters in the church at that time). My queer classmates and I tried to navigate the waters of seminary in a time when the question of whether we should even be there was considered fair game.

I thought that change was right around the corner, and for eight years after ordination I held on in the Presbyterian Church. Finally, I had to make a choice. Despite my deep love for the traditions and theology of the Presbyterian Church, I ended up transferring my ordination to a denomination where I could fully be myself.

Jesus tells a story about workers in a vineyard. Some started their work early in the day. Others came just before the work was done. When evening fell, the owner of the vineyard paid the workers who came late a full day's wages. The workers who had been there since the morning got excited. Surely they would get even more! Instead, they got the exact same pay. It didn't feel fair.

Twenty years after graduating from seminary, I opened Twitter to find that the national office of the Presbyterian Church had posted a rainbow flag in celebration of Pride month. You might think that I would be overjoyed by how far the church had come. Instead, I was furious.

"Don't you remember what you did to us?" I thought. "How dare you use our flag after the pain we endured while you decided whether we were worthy!"

Later that day I thought about that anger. I still carry some hurt from those days of exclusion, and I truly believe that every denomination that has excluded LGBTQ folks must do the work of apologizing and making amends. At the same time, I'm glad that today's queer and trans Presbyterian youth are growing up in a church that celebrates them.

Some of us come to the vineyards early, and others late, but at the end of the day it's the harvest that matters the most.

Prayer

God, when others take longer to get to work than I, remind me that a whole lot of others have been at work long before me. Amen.

Chapter 79

WHEN IT'S NOT OK

Out of the depths I cry to you, LORD; LORD, hear my voice. Let your ears be attentive to my cry for mercy.

—Psalm 130:1–2 NIV

My first call out of seminary was to a children's hospital. I was a chaplain in a pediatric emergency room, and I spent most of my time meeting with families on what were often the worst days of their lives.

The staff at that hospital were all exceptional. Thanks to them, most of the children who came through the trauma bay doors survived, and even thrived. But that was not always the case. And, for each family, for at least a little while, there was fear and pain and uncertainty.

I would sit with anxious parents while they waited for news. I always felt that it was a holy privilege. And I saw some extraordinary friends who would come and sit with them too, trying to give comfort. But, from time to time, sometimes a well-meaning friend would try a little too hard to make everything all right.

You've probably heard some of the things they said: "God meant this for a reason," or "God just needed another angel," or "God doesn't give you more than you can handle." It might have made the one saying it feel better for a minute, but it never seemed to help the parents much.

Most of us have probably heard something similar in our hours of greatest pain. We hear about injustice and friends assure us "it's not that bad." We lose a friend who could have been saved and are told, "Well, they made their choices." We get sick and cruel voices say, "It's God's punishment." All are meant to silence us in some way and keep others from the discomfort of sharing the pain.

One of the things I love about the Psalms is that they do not try to make it all better. Instead, they give us honesty. The writers talk about grief and pain and doubt. And, as the Psalmist wrote in today's verse, sometimes they even called to God "out of the depths" on the worst days of their life.

One day I was sitting with a crying mother whose daughter was in surgery after an act of senseless violence. A clearly uncomfortable friend tried to comfort her by saying, "It's all right." The mother closed her eyes, began to cry harder, and started to shout, "It's not all right . . . it's not all right!"

And, though her daughter would later recover, at that moment it wasn't all right. And, just like the Psalms, hers was one of the most honest prayers I have ever heard.

Prayer

Compassionate God, on those days when "out of the depths we cry to you," may you bless us with friends like the Psalmists, who are able to sit with us, and to cry out alongside us. Amen.

Chapter 80

SUBJECT

Wives, be subject to your husbands, as is fitting in the Lord. Husbands, love your wives and never treat them harshly.

—Colossians 3:18–19

Paul really gets it wrong sometimes. And this is one of those times. Wives, be subject to your husbands, he writes. And husbands, be nice to your wives. The idea of being kind to one another isn't the problem. It's the gendered and hierarchical nature of Paul's ideal marriage that's the trouble.

This passage, for obvious reasons, doesn't work for my marriage to my wife. Even if we were not a same-sex couple, it's still problematic. The idea that our gender, however we define it, somehow grants us authority in our marriage or commands our submission is fundamentally flawed. It is a relic of a different time, captured in a letter sent by a man of his time.

But there's one part of Paul's marital advice that does make sense to me: being subject to one another. I'm a strongly independent person, which is why the most sobering realization when I got married was that my choices would now affect my wife. Things I hadn't given a second thought to in the past now required conversations. Assumptions I made had to be checked.

The same, of course, was true for my wife. And that's the challenge, and the promise, of marriage. While the two people involved do not stop being individuals, they do become mutually subject, or responsible, to one another.

There was a time in my life when that loss of freedom terrified me. Now that I am married, I see it differently. I find tremendous freedom in the love of someone who wants to walk through this world together. The challenge of marriage is learning how to walk together in such a way where neither person feels like they are being dragged. Sometimes it's a lot tougher than going it alone, but in the end, I've never known greater joy.

Prayer

God, help me to value my connections with others more than I value my own way. Amen.

Chapter 81

UNHELPFUL HELPERS

"If one ventures a word with you, will you be offended?"

—Job 4:2

The remnants of a tropical storm found their way to the valley in Vermont where I pastored my first church. We were catastrophically flooded within hours. The rivers rushed their banks, picking up whole buildings and washing them downstream. The asphalt of the road was torn from the ground and tossed to the side by the water. When the rain stopped, we all walked into the town and stared in disbelief.

That's when the emails and phone calls and social media posts started.

"We'd like to come up and help!" said out-of-towners with no particular disaster-recovery skills. When local authorities asked them not to, in part because the devastated mountainous roads were literally crumbling, they said, "We're coming anyway."

"I have a whole truckload of clothes I've collected to donate," someone a few states away who had a ski home in the area posted on social media. When locals said that local thrift stores had already taken care of the few folks who had lost clothes, they were called "ungrateful."

Don't get me wrong—I'm sure these offers came with the best of intentions. The same was true when Job's friends tried to talk to him after he had lost everything, including his family. The only problem was that in neither case was it helpful.

Too often we want to "fix it." That urge often comes from our own feelings of helplessness and discomfort. Too seldom do we actually sit, listen, and hear what would really be helpful to those who hurt. Job's friends were doing just fine while they were sitting quietly with him, mouths shut. Then, not so much.

Even if we are members of the LGBTQ community, none of us encompasses all the identities that acronym includes. That means that sometimes even we queer and trans folks are in the position of being allies to other queer and trans folks whose identities do not match ours. Still, it can be tempting to think that we know the right solutions for the problems others face.

Sometimes I need to remind myself that my sage advice is about as good as a truckload of unneeded second-hand jean shorts, or that my one-size-fits-all solution that worked for me is as potentially dangerous as driving a station wagon up a disintegrating mountain road that everyone should be staying clear of. In these moments, I'm reminded that the best I can do is to pray for wisdom and wait for the ones at the center of the pain to tell me how to help (and how not to).

Prayer

God, when I want to save the day, help me to check my own wants so that I can truly meet other's needs. Amen.

Chapter 82

GETTING OUR
WORDS RIGHT

*I want their hearts to be encouraged and united
in love, so that they may have all the riches of
assured understanding and have the knowledge
of God's mystery, that is, Christ himself.*

—Colossians 2:2

I sat in a quiet corner of the student center watching
the clock. I wasn't going to back out. I was 18 and a
college freshman, and it was 1994 in the deep South.
This was the day that I was going to tell our college
chaplain, Sammy, a Methodist minister with a deep
Georgia accent, that I was gay.

I was ready for what would come. He was a kind
man, and I didn't think he would kick me out of the
Christian fellowship group. I did think he would say
I should pray, I should resist my attractions, I should
maybe even see a doctor who could change me.

Sitting in his office, the words came slow. He sat
in an armchair next to my own, and I looked forward,
afraid to catch his eyes. Occasionally, though, I'd see
him nodding. Finally, he got up, crossed over to a fil-
ing cabinet behind the desk, and pulled out a manilla
folder. He handed it to me and sat back down.

In it were articles from biblical scholars breaking down the "clobber texts" that were traditionally used to condemn same-sex attraction and exposing them as totally irrelevant to consensual adults. Sammy explained the differences between the context of Paul's letters and the present day. He talked about Sodom and how the real sin had not been gay sex, but inhospitality.

Finally, he said simply, "I affirm you."

I often think back on that day and wonder how differently my faith life would have turned out had I approached a minister who was not so wonderfully affirming. What if I had heard "love the sinner, hate the sin" or been told to "pray the gay away"?

I know that for so many LGBTQ folks that has been the case. The spiritual trauma they have faced has taken years to undo. That's why I give such deep thanks for those early voices of affirmation that at least some of us were able to hear and be steadied by.

I don't think Sammy woke up that day thinking that he would have such a positive impact on the teenager who would walk through his door. He probably didn't realize what he had done when he went to bed either. Through the years I'd hear from friends about how they too had gone to his office, told him their stories with fear and trembling, and received the same loving affirmation.

On any given day, none of us knows how our words might change a life, but surely they can. Thanks be to God for the days we get it right.

Prayer

God, when a knock comes on my door, help me to open it and to find the right words. Amen.

Chapter 83

COMPASSION FOR
THE BULLY

"Do to others as you would have them do to you."

—Luke 6:31

By seventh period each day, I was nearly done with another day of my terrible ninth grade year. First, though, I had to get through the toughest part of my day: Spanish class. It wasn't the verb conjugation or the fear of getting the alphabet wrong again (I never could roll my r's). It was the bully who sat behind me.

Every day would be the same. She'd whisper things over my shoulder, sometimes backed up by her football player friend. "Hey . . . is it true? Are you a dyke?" Sometimes I'd ignore it. Sometimes I'd deny it. She'd just keep going, "You're gay, aren't you?"

One day, after months of this, she grabbed the back of my bag in the hallway. I had never been in a fight in my life, but something in me snapped. I whirled around, anger in my eyes, fist clenched. She looked surprised, seemed to realize she was outmatched, let go and wandered off. She left me alone after that.

But in a real way she didn't leave me alone. For years I would think of her and feel angry. Then one day on Facebook, I saw her name pop up in the "people you may know" section. It was not long after the death of Tyler Clementi, who had been bullied to the point of suicide. Something welled up in me, and I hit the "message" button.

I recounted all she had done to me, told her I was now out and proud, and asked, "Why did you do that?" I was stunned when she responded back, "I would never make fun of anyone for being gay." I doubled down, recounting more specific incidents, telling her how she had made each hour of Spanish class a living hell for me.

This time the response took longer. She wrote back, saying she believed me, though she didn't remember it. She told me she'd already been deep into an addiction by ninth grade, and things were hazy. And then she told me the most shocking thing of all: she was gay too.

My anger began to melt away. I began to have empathy for that other queer kid growing up in a conservative Southern town who was deeply in pain. Before long, my pain was less intense. It still shouldn't have happened, but now I could start to let it go.

I told her I forgave her, was glad for her when she told me she was now clean and sober, and wished her well. I felt that finally that queer kid in me that had been so hurt was able to say, "It's OK now . . . it's done." She and I haven't talked since, but I do sincerely hope, wherever she is, that she has found love for that queer kid that still lives inside her.

Prayer

God, give me empathy. Even when I don't want to have it. Amen.

Chapter 84

TELLING THE TRUTH
ABOUT SIN

*Both we and our ancestors have sinned; we have
committed iniquity, have done wickedly.*

—Psalm 106:6

I was once giving a series of lectures to a wonderfully engaged group. It was clear that what I was saying was resonating as heads nodded and notes were taken. And then one day, I talked about sin, and the mood changed.

"It's so negative."

"Can't we use another word for it?"

"Saying that people sin sounds so, well, judgmental."

No one likes to talk about sin. Especially in the progressive church. We talk instead about making a mistake, or the wrong life choices. But we get squeamish when we are asked to call something, even if it's our own action, sinful.

I especially get that when writing for an audience of LGBTQ Christians and their friends. All of us have been called sinners for who we love, who we are, or who we support. We don't need more spiritual abuse. So first let me say, being exactly who you are and loving who you love is not a sin.

But even though we can be proud of who we are, we do indeed sin in hundreds of other ways. For queer and trans folks in the church, already so judged by the church, the pressure to be perfect is often higher than it is for others. The good news is that there is a freedom in being able to admit that sometimes we are imperfect, sometimes we fall short, and sometimes we do not act the way God would have us act.

The Harry Potter series taught us that "fear of the name only increases fear of the thing itself."[6] Sure, Dumbledore was talking about Voldemort, but the same thing applies to sin. If we get too afraid to even speak its name, it holds a certain fearful power over it.

And so, I say this freely: I'm a sinner. And so are you. And so are we all. Because none of us is perfect, and none of us always gets it right. In the end, sin is just shorthand for saying that sometimes our will and actions are not in full alignment with God's. But the good news is that God gives us the grace to know that, and the will to want to change that. For that, I am thankful.

Prayer

God, I know that I don't get it right sometimes. But I'm trying. Help me to never be too afraid to admit that. Amen.

Chapter 85

THE GREATEST

*At that time the disciples came to Jesus and asked,
"Who is the greatest in the kingdom of heaven?"
Then he called a little child over to sit among the
disciples, and said, "I assure you that if you don't
turn your lives around and become like this little child,
you will definitely not enter the kingdom of heaven.
Those who humble themselves like this little child
will be the greatest in the kingdom of heaven."*

—Matthew 18:1–4 CEB

Humility isn't in vogue in our culture. Even more than competence, outright hubris can now win the day. Humility is for losers with low self-esteem, and we love winners.

But what might win elections and promotions is not what wins God's heart. Jesus rejects those who are seeking to be "the greatest" and instead opens his arms up to those who "humble themselves" like children.

In certain circles I've traveled in, ones where power and privilege are not the norm, I've heard the concept of humility dismissed. I understand why. But being proud and being humble are not opposites. You can, and should, absolutely believe that you are a beloved child of God, created by God and profoundly gifted. No one is inherently more worthy than you.

But the problem comes when you begin to believe that you are more worthy than others.

True humility is not about thinking of yourself as less than others. True humility is knowing that you are equally worthy, and that every good gift you have been given is not for yourself but for others.

What we learned as children, and somehow better understood, about how to treat one another still applies. And even if it doesn't win the day in the board room or on the ballot, that child-like virtue still wins God's heart every time.

Prayer

God, help me to love myself exactly as you made me, and help me to be humble enough to love others well. Amen.

Chapter 86

SAINTS IN TRAINING

They will hunger no more, and thirst no more; the sun
will not strike them, nor any scorching heat; for the
Lamb at the center of the throne will be their shepherd,
and he will guide them to springs of the water of life,
and God will wipe away every tear from their eyes.

—Revelation 7:16–17

Martin Luther famously said that while we live we are all simultaneously saints and sinners. We are imperfect and messy, prone to doing all the wrong things, and completely hapless. And yet, we are also the beloved children of God, trying every day to get it just a little more right. In other words, we are human beings who are alive.

Many mainline Protestant traditions believe something else too. We believe that when we die, we join the Communion of Saints. Far from a club for people who lived perfect lives, or believed without doubt, sainthood is a state achieved not by works but by dying in the hope of Christ's grace and love.

That means that one day we will all be saints. It also means that there already exists a gathering of queer and trans saints who have lived and died before us. Beyond just their examples, powerful enough, we know that there is a crowd gathered in the next life of those who have already gone before us, and that is now cheering us on. One day, we too will be a part of it.

For now, though, we are simply saints in training. Like any other learners, we will often get it wrong. We will stumble and cause pain. We will behave in decidedly unsaintly ways. And yet, we will continue to move forward, closer to sainthood with each breath.

This day, how will you become just a little more saint-like? What will you do differently? How will you claim the title that will one day be given to you?

There will come a day when every tear this life brings will be wiped away, and fear will be no more. On that day, sainthood will be less joyless perfection and more a celebration of God's grace and goodness. Maybe for those of us who are on this side of sainthood that means that today is a great day to start practicing joy.

Prayer

God, help me learn to be a saint. But not too soon, God, and not too perfectly. Amen.

Chapter 87

THE DIVINE BAKER

*And again [Jesus] said, "To what should I
compare the kingdom of God? It is like yeast
that a woman took and mixed in with three
measures of flour until all of it was leavened."*

—Luke 13:20–21

I'm not a great cook but I love watching cooks work.
I especially love bakers who carefully mix their ingredients one by one before magically turning a bowl of
dough into something beautiful.

I once was watching a baker mix the ingredients
using some sort of kitchen tool. I had no idea what
the contraption was but she explained it to me. The
idea is that all the ingredients are put in it and mixed
together so that they are more evenly distributed. The
result is a better quality, more consistent, bread or
pastry.

When Jesus was describing the kingdom of God,
he talked about mixing yeast and flour. On its own,
flour does not amount to much, but with a little yeast it
becomes good bread. But first, it all needs to be mixed
together so that the whole loaf will be leavened.

That's what the kingdom of God is like. Even
when we are feeling as bland as plain old flour, it only
takes a little bit of the holy to perk us up and create

us into something wonderful, and something that can feed the world.

Too often the church has debated the full inclusion of queer and trans people in a way that centered the question on whether we should be allowed in the mix at all. What they've missed is that, far from spoiling the recipe, we have something to add that can make it extraordinary. God created us not to be made like everyone else, but to stand out and bring new depth and flavor to the goodness of creation.

To dare to be added to the mix is no small act of courage for LGBTQ folks. To be part of the church, to bring our gifts, is to be willing to be shaken up, to coexist with others nothing like us, and to say that we want to let the divine baker form us into something even more wonderful than we already are. That is a tall order sometimes. But anything else is only about as exciting as plain old crackers. And you were meant to be rainbow cake.

Prayer

God, thank you for letting us be an ingredient in the divine recipe you are creating. Amen.

Chapter 88

PLANS

Come now, you who say, "Today or tomorrow we will go to such and such a town and spend a year there, doing business and making money." Yet you do not even know what tomorrow will bring. What is your life? For you are a mist that appears for a little while and then vanishes. Instead you ought to say, "If the Lord wishes, we will live and do this or that."

—James 4:13–15

I'm pretty good at making long-term plans. This is not new to me. By the time I was nine I had my life trajectory planned out. I was going to go to the Naval Academy and become a pilot. Nothing was going to stop me.

So, none of that happened. And that's probably for the best because it turns out I really don't like flying that much. But that doesn't stop me from mapping out my future. I have plans for writing, plans for ministry, and plans for a retirement that's still decades away.

But here's what I've found about my plans: God often interrupts them with something better. For instance, I thought I would spend my entire ministry in the Deep South, and instead I wind up a New Englander. Or, I said I would never pastor a church, but then I fell in love with pastoral ministry. Or, I decided marriage is probably not for me, and then I fell head-over-heels for the woman who became my wife.

James reminds us that we are good at making plans, but we aren't so good at knowing our limits. By that I don't mean that we aren't aware enough of the hundreds of things that can go wrong. Instead, I mean that too often we have had views of our future that are way too limited. We don't know what doors God is going to open for us. And we have no clue how we will end up underestimating God's plans for us.

So instead, what would it be like to set a new agenda that includes only this: "If the Lord wishes, we will live and do this or that." For all of us planners, it may be terrifying for a while, but I'll bet it will be worth the ride.

Prayer

Dear God, help us to clear our agendas and hand them over to you. Amen.

Chapter 89

LAUGHABLE

*Then one of the men said, "I will definitely return
to you about this time next year. Then your wife
Sarah will have a son!" . . . So Sarah laughed to
herself, thinking, I'm no longer able to have children
and my husband's old. The Lord said to Abraham,
"Why did Sarah laugh and say, 'Me give birth? At
my age?' Is anything too difficult for the Lord?"*

—Genesis 18:10–14 CEB

Abraham and Sarah had given up on having children
together. Years past the age of fertility, they knew it
just wasn't possible. So when Sarah hears that she is
going to have a child, her response is a natural one:
she laughs.

But God asks, "Why are you laughing? Is anything too difficult for me?" And within the year,
Abraham and Sarah have a son named Isaac, which
loosely translated means "to laugh."

It is important to acknowledge that Abraham and
Sarah's infertility wasn't a result of their own lack of
effort or belief. It wasn't, and plenty of faithful people
struggle with starting families.

But too often, in all sorts of situations, like Sarah,
we laugh off what is possible. And even worse, unlike

Sarah, we laugh off what is possible not just for ourselves, but also for others.

I was once talking to a woman who had an ambition to be a doctor as a child. When she told her parents, they laughed. "Who ever heard of a girl being a doctor?" they asked. Her dream was, literally, laughable. She did not become a doctor, and she still remembers that day as the one when she started to think her dream was pretty laughable too.

Growing up, I didn't have the words yet to describe who I was as a queer and non-binary person. I just knew I was different from almost everyone I saw. I couldn't imagine a life, let alone one that could be full of joy. It was almost laughable. But nothing is too wonderful for God. The world began to change, I met others who showed me what life could look like, and I did a little stepping out in faith and creating a space for myself that did not yet exist. Now I look back and laugh at how God has broken open the world again and again.

When I work with the children and youth of my church, I'm always aware of the power I hold to shape their futures. I try to remember that an offhand comment might squelch a kid's dream. Some might say that is a form of coddling, but I don't think that's true.

Instead, I see it as staying out of God's way. God gives each of us untold potential. If we are fortunate, we learn to listen for signs of it early on. When the next generation is doing their own listening, the last thing I want them to hear is the laughter of those who believe some things are indeed too difficult for the Lord.

Prayer

God, help me to laugh not at dreams, but at doubts. Amen.

Chapter 90

COMING HOME

"If you return, O Israel, says the
LORD, if you return to me. . . ."

—Jeremiah 4:1a

The call to repent is always fairly unsettling. When-
ever we hear someone talking about repentance,
there's always a sense that some sort of judgment is
going on. Someone, somewhere, has determined that
we're in need of a change of heart.

Queer and trans folks have for too long heard
loud Christian voices calling on us to repent. We've
been asked to suppress the people God has created
us to be to better fit into what others feel comfortable
with. It's no wonder that when we hear people talk
about sin and repentance, our first instinct is often to
run the other way.

But repentance doesn't have to be scary. That's
especially true if we hear what "repentance" really
means. If you go back to the root of the Greek word
for it that's found in the original text of the New Testament, you find that the word is *metanoia*. Metanoia
is roughly translated as "to change your mind." It's a
call to think differently. A call not just to change your
mind, but a call to change your actions as well.

This repentance isn't about feeling bad or ashamed or guilty, and it's in no way about denying who we are as queer and trans folks. Instead, it's about being fully ourselves. It's about being willing to put aside the things that are keeping us from fully participating in what comes next. It's about believing that our mistakes and our past don't have to define our future. And it's about deciding to believe that we can be a part of God's own work in our world.

But, most of all, repentance is not about beating ourselves up for being bad people. It's about deciding to come home to God once again.

When Jesus talks about a father who ran as fast as he could to welcome his prodigal son, he was really repeating an old story. Throughout Scripture, the theme is the same. Again and again, God calls for us to change our minds and come home once again. Home to a place where there is no judgment, but only open arms. Home to a place where we will always be welcome, no matter how many times we stray.

Prayer

Holy God, help us to remember how to come home, and help us to dare to turn around and start the journey back. Amen.

Chapter 91

REFUSING TO SHRINK BACK

But recall those earlier days when, after you had
been enlightened, you endured a hard struggle
with sufferings, sometimes being publicly exposed
to abuse and persecution, and sometimes being
partners with those so treated. . . . My soul takes
no pleasure in anyone who shrinks back.

—Hebrews 10:32–33, 38b

On June 26, 2015, I was sitting in a hotel conference room in Cleveland with a group of other clergy. I was trying to pay attention to the speaker but, to be honest, I was obsessively refreshing my Twitter feed. The Supreme Court of the United States was about to let the world know if the marriages of countless same-sex couples would now be legal across the land, including my own.

An older minister once told me about a lecture he had attended as a young student. Karl Barth, perhaps the most eminent theologian of the twentieth century, was speaking. A student got up and asked him, "What is the nature of church?" According to the minister, Barth responded, "The church is wherever two or more are gathered, and you are understood at your deepest level."

The moment the Supreme Court decision reached us in Cleveland, the entire room broke out into applause, tears, and praise. We prayed together, and we sang the doxology.

In that room were a number of married LGBTQ people who had just been fully understood by the law of the land for the first time in their lives. And there were also allies, who understood what that moment meant for us at our deepest level. It was church. And it was church when later that day my wife and I embraced on the streets of Cleveland, a place where hours before our marriage had not been recognized.

Because good people of faith refused to "shrink back," both in our churches and in our country, so many of us are not lost. We can now be known at our deepest levels in so many places. I am so thankful for that, and for all those people of faithful courage. And in the struggles still to come, I hope I can do the same for others.

Prayer

Dear God, thank you for knowing us at our deepest level, and for loving us. And thank you for those who refuse to shrink back from doing the same. Amen.

Chapter 92

PROVOKED

And let us consider how to provoke one another to
love and good deeds, not neglecting to meet together,
as is the habit of some, but encouraging one another,
and all the more as you see the Day approaching.

—Hebrews 10:24–25

Have you ever heard someone say, "I was provoked"? Sometimes you hear it as a defense after a fight: "He provoked me!" The idea is that whatever response they had was somehow justified.

That's why I've always thought of being provoked as something negative, or as an attempted excuse for violence. Because at the end of the day, you can't blame someone else for your own bad behavior.

But what about the other side? What about being provoked to do good?

The author of Hebrews tells readers that they can "provoke one another to love and good deeds." They can be encouragers who gather in community to lift one another up.

In my twenties I had a mentor who provoked me. The first openly queer clergy person I knew, she provoked me to do the right thing, to live a life of gratitude, and to serve God first. She provoked me to want to be a better person. How? By simply being herself, a good and kind and decent person who encouraged others and expected the best of them.

Would I be the person I am today had I not met her? My guess is probably not. Twenty-year-old me needed a little provocation in the right direction, and by God's grace I got it.

But for too many, the spiritual journey is one that is walked in isolation. And without the loving provocation of good people of faith, the angry provocations of a harsh world can be overwhelming.

Our job as followers of Christ in community is to provoke one another with kindness, with compassion, with loving challenges, and with encouragement. Because ours is a provocative faith, in the best sense of the word.

Prayer

O God, provoke me, that I may provoke others, and that we may provoke the world. Amen.

Chapter 93

SETTING OUR SIGHTS

When the days drew near for him to be taken up, he set his face to go to Jerusalem.

—Luke 9:51

When I was in seminary, I read Scripture at the wedding of a good friend and classmate of mine. One of the readings was this passage from Luke. Although I applauded the fact that my friend had veered from the typical "love is patient, love is kind" reading, I have to admit it felt kind of odd.

When the pastor started preaching, she concentrated on this verse: "And he set his face to go to Jerusalem." At first, I had no idea why this was an appropriate wedding verse. This is about Jesus choosing to go to Jerusalem and toward the certain death he knew awaited him when he arrived. Not so cheerful for a wedding day.

But now, married myself, I get it. I don't mean that marriage means death. (Honestly, honey, I don't.) But I do know now how much marriage means deciding to be married and focusing on that decision together. It means setting your sights on the covenant you make with your partner and keeping your eyes on the prize.

I think that's true of any commitment we decide to make, especially when it comes to being in any kind of relationship with others. There are always times of challenge, always times of frustration, and always times of change. Christ knew those were coming when he set his sights on Jerusalem.

But, despite all that, there are far more times of joy, redemption, and grace along the way. If you let yourself look away, you will never see them. But if you set your sights on what matters most, you'll be surprised how even the most serious of commitments can feel life-giving. Even in the hardest times.

Prayer

God, help us to set our sights on Jerusalem, and may you always be in our vision. Amen.

Chapter 94

READ TOGETHER

Now there was an Ethiopian eunuch. . . . He had
come to Jerusalem to worship and was returning
home; seated in his chariot, he was reading the
prophet Isaiah. Then the Spirit said to Philip, "Go
over to this chariot and join it." So Philip ran up to it
and heard him reading the prophet Isaiah. He asked,
"Do you understand what you are reading?"

—Acts 8:27–30

I was an English major in college. One of the degree
requirements was to take a class centered on a text
written in Middle English. I chose Chaucer's *Canter-
bury Tales*, and for the next semester I stumbled over
passage after passage, supposedly written in the language I spoke.

Truth be told, much of the time I didn't understand what I was reading.

I have felt that way about the Bible from time to
time too. In fact, I used to be far more afraid of the
Bible than I was of Chaucer. As a newly out Christian, I would approach the Bible only fearfully, thinking that it contained passages that would send me
straight to hell.

The difference between Chaucer and Scripture,
though, is that I kept coming back to Scripture. In

large part that was because I found communities that would read with me, and ways that we could grow and share our understandings of the text with one another. Being part of a group of other Christians who read the Bible means that we will read passages multiple times in a lifetime. They will be a part of the larger fabric of our lives.

And if we are lucky, someone might come up to us the same way Philip did and ask, "Do you understand what you are reading?"

They probably won't do it exactly like that. Instead, they'll live their life in such a way that it illustrates what the Scriptures mean when they talk about God's love and grace. Or they'll break open the Scripture by offering a story or example that helps us to really get what the Bible says. They will make the text less frightening and more wondrous. And, hopefully, at times we will do the same for others.

We read Scripture in community because sometimes we need one another to understand. As much as the personal study of Scripture is valuable and instructive, sometimes we just need to put our heads together and explain to one another what we understand it to mean. The Bible is, at its core, a communal text, meant to be read in community, and meant to gather the community around itself.

Sharing it with one another is what keeps it from being just another semi-understood book, right there on the shelf next to our old copy of Chaucer.

Prayer

God, thank you for giving us your Word, and thank you for giving us one another. Help us to look to one another to better understand it. Amen.

Chapter 95

DISPATCHES FROM THE PIT

*Answer me quickly, O Lord; my spirit fails.
Do not hide your face from me, or I shall be
like those who go down to the Pit. Let me
hear of your steadfast love in the morning.*

—Psalm 143:7–8a

The month I turned 22, I was in the middle of a years-long fight against clinical depression. I had my college degree in hand (double major in four years), I was starting a new graduate program (seminary, no less), and I had loving friends and family. I had everything to live for, and yet, I was fighting against soul-crushing feelings of hopelessness and sadness every day. I thought something must be spiritually wrong with me. After all, if you love God, and believe in the love and grace of Christ, how can you not be joyful? I believed that as a Christian I was a failure.

Years, nearly decades, later I tell this story publicly with some trepidation. There is still a profound stigma about mental illness. It is the same stigma I carried with me at 22. I saw my clinical depression as a moral failure, something bad that was happening to me because I was not strong enough to will myself well.

I didn't know then about how my particular brain chemistry made it hard for my serotonin to be reabsorbed, for instance. I didn't know that in any given year 6.7 percent of American adults are currently suffering through a clinical depression. I didn't know that LGBTQ folks suffer from higher rates of mental illness, in large part due to the stigma and trauma we often face. I also didn't know that many of the people I looked up to and respected, including many clergy members, had gone through the same thing, or something similar. Which is why I tell you this now.

Depression tells many lies. One of them is that we are somehow beneath God's love. But it just is not true. God knows us, and God knows when we suffer. God loves us immensely in those moments, and I truly believe God wants healing for us.

The job of the church is not to create stigmas that keep people from getting help. It's to break those stigmas apart and offer God's hope. If you are suffering, don't listen to the lies of the disease. Instead, listen to God's hope. And then, make the phone call for help that you've been putting off. Fill that antidepressant prescription you said you'd never need. Tell your pastor, or your friends.

Queer, trans, or something else entirely, you are a beloved child of God. You deserve to feel that way.

Prayer

God, as your people may we break down the stigmas of this world and proclaim the wonder of each of your children. Amen.

Chapter 96

THE GIFTS OF
THE DISAGREEABLE

I urge you to watch out for people who create divisions and problems against the teaching that you learned. Keep away from them. People like that aren't serving the Lord. They are serving their own feelings. They deceive the hearts of innocent people with smooth talk and flattery.

—Romans 16:17–18 CEB

Journalist and author Malcolm Gladwell has a theory. He believes that the people who truly create social change in this world are always a little "disagreeable." Far from people who seek peace and unity at all costs, disagreeable people are willing not to be liked by everyone. They are also willing to break a rule from time to time to do what is right.

We don't like conflict in churches. I certainly understand why. As a pastor, I used to hold my breath during church meetings when there were differences in opinions. I didn't want there to be a fight. In recent years, though, I've begun to understand that differences of opinion are not just OK, but even vital. If a group starts thinking with one mind, and no one is ever willing to object, that is a sign that there is a huge problem.

Are there people who like to "create divisions and problems"? Absolutely. We've all known church bullies who love to start drama. But should everyone who has a different opinion be put in that category? No. In fact, far too often the church has labeled those who push for inclusion or equality as simply being contrary or troublesome. The danger in that is that if the church plugs its ears to the still-speaking voice of God that comes through the voices of each generation, the church will never progress any further in the advancement of God's vision than it has so far.

Paul warns the church in Rome to be on the lookout for anyone who contradicts the truths that they know. He tells them to be aware of the ones who serve themselves and not God. It is the deception of God's people that he is worried about; not the threat of a disagreeable person who is still trying to stay in community and find God's will.

The next time that a contradictory opinion comes up in your church, test the spirits. Is it really a "division and problem"? Or is it possible that it's another way of understanding what God is doing in your church? God speaks from the margins more than we know, and maybe that disagreeable voice is a sign that the still-speaking God has something new to say.

Prayer

God, help me to hear what you are telling the church today, no matter whose voice you are using, and help me to test the spirits of all I hear. Amen.

Chapter 97

TAKING NOTICE

*The LORD said, "I've been paying close attention
to you and to what has been done to you in Egypt.
I've decided to take you away from the harassment
in Egypt to the land of the Canaanites, the Hittites,
the Amorites, the Perizzites, the Hivites, and the
Jebusites, a land full of milk and honey."*

—Exodus 3:16b–18 CEB

Do you ever feel like God is not paying attention? I've
felt that way before. Sometimes I'll look at the unfair-
ness of the world, and the way that evil seems to win
out, and I'll wonder, "Doesn't God care?"

In the midst of their captivity in Egypt, my guess
is that the Israelites wondered that too. Where was
God? Why wasn't God doing anything? How much
longer did they have to remain here, building the Pha-
raoh's city?

People sometimes ask me why God doesn't seem
to care about injustice. Doesn't God know that people
are suffering? It's a fair question. When we watch the
news, God feels so far away.

I used to tell people that God does know what
is happening, and that God is right there with those
who suffer the most, surrounding them with compassion and love. I think that is true, but I'm not sure

how helpful that was for the people I met. Today it feels a little too glib and easy an answer.

Jesus once said that a sparrow doesn't fall to the earth without God knowing. If that's true, I think God knows when we are in pain, when the unjust gain power, or when things feel hopeless. I think good does, indeed, pay close attention.

I sometimes wonder if God's not just paying attention to what is happening, though, but to how we are responding. How are we confronting the evils of this world? When are we standing up for others and when are we standing back?

I believe there will be a time when God will lead us into a "land full of milk and honey." I believe that because I believe in a God who pays attention. I sometimes wonder, though, whether God might be waiting for us to signal that we are ready. When we start to participate in the liberation of one another, maybe then, when God knows we are truly ready to move to the promised land, God will make a way out for us all.

Prayer

God, please keep paying close attention, and please help us get ready to move. Amen.

Chapter 98

NOTHING

For I am convinced that neither death, nor life, nor angels, nor rulers, nor things present, nor things to come, nor powers, nor height, nor depth, nor anything else in all creation, will be able to separate us from the love of God in Christ Jesus our Lord.

—Romans 8:38–39

Some spiritual writers have talked about *thin places*. These are the spaces (literally and metaphorically) where it feels like the veil between our world and the next is barely there, and God's love may easily be felt. Years ago, a friend who was going through a traumatic loss asked me, is there such a thing as a *thick place*, a place where God feels as distant as another universe?

I believe many of us do some time in thick places. God's love feels like an absurd abstraction that we can't believe exists. Even in our best moments there, we might believe that God's love is real, but surely it exists only for other people.

So many queer and trans Christians know that place. It's easy to trust the loudest voices around us more than the quiet yet constant voice of the Holy Spirit. There are days even still where the homophobic and transphobic words of Christian preachers pierce me, and old fears of losing God's love come back.

It's ironic that it is Paul, whose words have so often been used or twisted to harm us, who reminds us that there is nothing in this world with the power to cut us off from God. Not who we are. Not who we love. Not which church accepts or rejects us. Not even the finality of death.

This world is full of thick places. Thankfully it also has many thin places. There's one sort of place it does not have, though: disconnected places. There is no place in this life or the next that God's love does not pierce, no human made barrier of exclusion that it cannot break down, and no hate-filled words that it cannot out-voice.

When this life is over, and the final layers of the veil are pulled back, God's love will be what guides us home. On that day all the distractions will fall away, and only that familiar love will remain with us. And we will, as always, be inseparable.

Prayer

God, nothing, absolutely nothing, can stop your love. On the days that feels hardest to believe, use that love to call me close. Amen.

Chapter 99

UNDERDOGS

[Samuel] looked on Eliab and thought, "Surely the LORD's anointed is now before the LORD." But the LORD said to Samuel, "Do not look on his appearance or on the height of his stature, because I have rejected him; for the LORD does not see as mortals see; they look on the outward appearance, but the LORD looks on the heart."

—1 Samuel 16:6–7

After the death of King Saul, God sent the prophet Samuel to look for the new king at the house of a man named Jesse. Jesse had seven older sons, a number that was considered blessed in the culture of his time. They were strong and tall, fit for the throne, and when Samuel saw them, he just knew that one of them had to be the new king.

One by one Jesse called his sons forward. But God spoke to Samuel as each approached: "Not that one. Not that one either. Nope, not him." God told Samuel not to look at the outside of each man, but to instead look at their heart. It went on like this until Samuel had seen each of the seven sons rejected by God. Exasperated, he asked Jesse, "Are these all your boys?"

Jesse admitted, "No, there's another—but he's the youngest and we left him to tend the sheep" (see 1 Sam. 16:11). Samuel calls him in, and God makes it clear: this runt of the litter, the eighth who spoiled the perfect seven, the one they hadn't even bothered to invite in the house—he is the king.

Too often we underestimate people for superficial reasons. We may not mean harm. Jesse probably just thought there was no way his youngest son could be the king with seven older brothers who seemed destined for greatness. Someone had to stay and watch the sheep, after all.

I've certainly been left standing out in the fields at times. You probably have too. For those of us who have, God brings good news. That's not where we have to stay. In every generation, God sends messengers who call us in, who proclaim us worthy, and who raise us up to the place where God has called us. And then, God calls us to do the same for others.

So often, God chooses the unexpected to do God's work. Should it be any surprise, then, that God might have something wonderful waiting for you?

Prayer

God, thank you for those who look on the heart, and thank you for the good hearts that you have given us. Amen.

Chapter 100

MORE LIGHT

The light shines in the darkness,
and the darkness did not overcome it.

—John 1:5

Four hundred years ago in a church in the Netherlands, a pastor named John Robinson preached to a congregation that included those who would travel on the Mayflower to the shores of Plymouth, Massachusetts (stopping first, notably, in Provincetown, which has the highest proportion of LGBTQ people per zip code). He told them that he believed God had "more truth and light" yet to be revealed.[7]

Those Pilgrims, and their Puritan siblings, would get a lot of things horribly wrong over the next centuries. Some of their spiritual heirs, though, would keep trying. They would turn back from hatred, turn toward justice, and work to come closer to revealing the true fullness of timeless truths. Despite the many messes that humans can create, God has used us even still. And, more importantly, God has loved us even still.

As we reach our last day together, I want to share a hope with you. I sincerely hope that this book will be outdated within about ten years if not less, God willing.

I say that because over two decades ago I was given a similar book of Christian devotionals, then labeled for "gays and lesbians." It was wonderfully written and deeply nourishing to my spirit, and I give thanks for having had it. It is also now, all these years later, incredibly dated.

The world has changed for queer folks, and for the better. It has changed even more for trans folks, who for too many years received less than even crumbs. I pray that this change continues, and that there will come a day when a new writer opens this book, reads something I wrote about LGBTQ folks or sexuality or gender, and cringes a little, and thinks "I'm so glad we understand more now."

We have not yet understood the fullness of God's truth and light. Perhaps we never will on this side of creation. But the light continues to shine in the darkness for us all, and the darkness will never overcome it.

Prayer

God, let your light break forth into my heart and into your world. Amen.

NOTES

Chapter 21

1. Indigo Girls, "Three County Highway," by Amy Ray, track 4 on *Despite Our Differences*, Hollywood Records, 2006.

Chapter 57

2. Alice Walker, *The Color Purple* (New York: Harcourt, 2003), 197.

Chapter 68

3. Harper Lee, *Go Set a Watchman* (New York: Harper Collins, 2015), 245.

Chapter 72

4. Martin Luther King Jr., "Steeler Lecture" (lecture, Dexter Avenue Baptist Church, Montgomery, AL, November 1967).

Chapter 76

5. Walter Wink, *Naming the Powers: The Language of Power in the New Testament* (Philadelphia: Fortress Press, 1984).

Chapter 84

6. J. K. Rowling, *Harry Potter and the Sorcerer's Stone* (New York: Scholastic Inc., 1997), 298.

Chapter 100

7. John Robinson, *The Works of John Robinson*, vol. 1 (London: John Snow, 1851). From a sermon delivered July 21, 1620, on the ship *Speedwell*, in port in Delft Haven, Holland. The Pilgrims were departing for England and then Massachusetts.

THEMATIC INDEX